FOREWORD BY ALISTAIR BEGG

A GOOD OLD AGE

AN **A TO Z**
OF LOVING AND FOLLOWING
THE LORD JESUS IN LATER YEARS

DEREK PRIME

10 Publishing
a division of 10 ofthose.com

Copyright © 2017 by Derek Prime

First published in Great Britain in 2017
Reprinted 2018

British Library Cataloguing in Publication Data
A record for this book is available from the British Library

ISBN: 978-1-911272-82-3

Designed and typeset by Pete Barnsley (CreativeHoot.com)

Printed in Denmark by Nørhaven

10Publishing, a division of 10ofthose.com
Unit C, Tomlinson Road, Leyland, PR25 2DY, England

Email: info@10ofthose.com
Website: www.10ofthose.com

CONTENTS

FOREWORD

The song writer Paul Simon describes, in 'Old Friends', how strange it is, while still in our youth, to imagine being seventy, and pictures two old men quietly sharing a park bench. When Paul penned these words, he was just twenty-seven. Now in the middle of his eighth decade, he has discovered what he had found hard to imagine, namely old age! He is not alone in viewing the prospect of ageing with uncertainty and fear. There is something unsettling about the general desolations of old age. As Derek Kidner writes in his commentary *The Message of Ecclesiastes*, 'old friends are taken, familiar customs change, and long-held hopes now have to be abandoned.' We need help in coming to terms with old age and learning how to handle it. And that is what we find in this book – that and so much more. There is something of the spirit of Caleb (who at eighty-five was still going strong) embedded in these pages. Instead of succumbing to the temptation to slow to a crawl, we are encouraged to run the race, looking to Jesus, right through the tape, all the way to the end.

The truths unpacked in these pages come from the pen of one who had begun to live by them long before he heard the bell ring for the final lap. It is an immense privilege to write this foreword because there is no living person to whom I owe more by way of godly pastoral wisdom and example than Derek Prime. Forty-two years ago I enjoyed the privilege of serving as 'assistant to the pastor' at Charlotte Chapel, Edinburgh. That I provided little by way of assistance is matter for another time. I was twenty-three and Derek appeared to me to be a much older man. It is quite sobering to realise that he was then twenty years younger than I am now.

Nothing in the book surprises me because the path he lays out for old age was one on which he was already walking in his middle years. He was a stickler for time, taking seriously Paul's exhortation to always be 'making the best use of the time' (Eph. 5:16, ESV). Our elders' meetings began and ended on time. We went up into the pulpit neither early nor late. To this day his sense of discipline, attention to detail and concern in it all for the glory of God and the well-being of His people is the standard to which I aspire.

My only concern in reading this material is that it will be housed in the wrong section of the library – geriatric studies. It needs to be read long before we find ourselves in the senior-citizen seats on the train. We want to be like those who were 'still living by faith when they died' (Heb. 11:13). In other words, those people of faith were still doing in the closing chapter what they had been doing throughout the course of their lives. They had not adopted a new pattern at the end, driven by guilt or fear; instead, seeing the finishing line in view, they had picked up the pace. Surely it is a life of humble dependency and steady consistency that paves the way to *A Good Old Age*.

Alistair Begg,
Senior Pastor at Parkside Church in Cleveland, Ohio.

A SUGGESTION TO THE READER

This is probably not a book best read in one go, but rather read a chapter a day for one month, and then repeated over other months if it is found helpful. You may probably wonder why I make this suggestion. Each chapter tries to establish a Christian imperative, that is to say an urgent and important priority for every day of our life as an old person. But the truth is that we cannot helpfully try to take on board twenty-six priorities all at once!

I have found that each of these priorities needs to be quietly considered and pondered one at a time, and then, hopefully, prayed about and increasingly made part of my Christian life. But each chapter may be thought of as being like condensed milk or undiluted orange squash – you shouldn't attempt to absorb it in that concentrated format! So my suggestion is to read a chapter a day and then add the water of your own prayers and thoughts to make it easier to digest.

INTRODUCTION

Old age may alarm us. It can bring humiliating experiences. Some of its limitations may take away our natural dignity. Worse still is the daunting possibility of dementia, even to the point where we may not remember our own name.

But, while there may be bad old age, when we feel 'weighed down with years' (Jer. 6:11), there is 'a good old age' (Gen. 25:8) to which we may aspire. Every period of life has its appointed benefits and excellence (Prov. 20:29).

The problems we encounter in old age are not new. I may become frail and stooped and have an increasing number of wrinkles. My skin may become thin, translucent and vulnerable. My ankles may swell and throb, and my legs experience frightening cramp in the night. I may have to depend upon a walking frame to get about my home. My brittle bones may make me afraid of falling. Ecclesiastes 12 tells a similar story. But while reaching seventy is a good life span, our years will never be without their troubles: 'their span is but trouble and sorrow, for they quickly pass, and we fly away' (Ps. 90:10).

Perils to avoid

When we reach old age, we are in danger of making several mistakes:

Pretending old age is not creeping up on us. When a son described his mother as entering upon the evening of her life, she interjected, 'Not evening, early afternoon!'

Always comparing the present with the past. As the Bible advises us, 'Do not say, "Why were the old days better than these?" For it is not wise to ask such questions' (Ecc. 7:10).

Mistrust. This raises its ugly head when we become suspicious of the motives of those who care for us, or sadly distrust our children or close relatives.

Pessimism. The subjects of pessimism are countless: our government, the state of the

Church – and perhaps sometimes our local church fellowship – and world events in general.

Self-pity. This is the saddest peril, for it is difficult for friends and relatives to cope with us when we are sorry for ourselves and only pour out our troubles every time we see them. Wallowing in self-pity indicates we have taken our eyes off God and His goodness to us.

Wonderful potential to embrace

In fact, old age can be the most fruitful period of our life (Ps. 92:14; 103:5). An important part of that fruitfulness is the ability to give **good and wise counsel**, not presuming to say, 'I know all the answers,' but rather, 'I know God-honouring principles that have best guided me in life.' Younger people are able to apply the principles we share in a way that is appropriate for them.

To the end of our life we may discover the **good works** God has prepared for us to do in whatever circumstances we find ourselves, both expected and unexpected. How sad it is if we so regret not doing what we have so much enjoyed doing *in the past* that we fail to see what God has for us to do *in the present*.

One area of good works in old age is becoming spiritual baggage-minders. Let me explain. David established the principle that his front-line soldiers and their baggage-minders were of equal value: 'The share of the man who stayed with the supplies is to be the same as that of him who went down to the battle. All shall share alike' (1 Sam. 30:24). We need to hold on to this truth in our old age. Younger Christians living out their faith may be considered the front-line fighters, but older people at home should be their spiritual baggage-minders. Every pastor, teacher, elder, deacon, evangelist, Sunday-school teacher, youth worker, missionary and Christian employee needs the support, encouragement and prayers of older believers who have already run the same race.

Old age is also a unique opportunity for **intercession**. We have more time to pray than before, and we have trodden many of the paths of those for whom we pray.

All these aspects mean that in old age we may even be identified as vital members of the body of Christ: 'those parts of the body that seem to be weaker are indispensable' (1 Cor. 12:22).

Truths to hold on to in old age

How, then, can we ensure that we grasp the positive possibilities of old age, rather than succumb to dwelling on its limitations? I suggest we remind ourselves of the following great biblical truths.

First is the amazing **forgiveness** that is ours in the Lord Jesus. Satan, the great enemy of souls, has the power to stir up the memory of old sins of which we are thoroughly ashamed. We should have a greater appreciation of our sinfulness in old age (John 8:7–9). At the age I am, I reflect much upon the past and the way God has helped, guided and blessed me, but at the same time I remember some of the stupid and sinful things I did when I was young. The wonder of God's grace is that He says to us, 'I, even I, am he who blots out your transgressions, for my own sake, and remembers your sins no more' (Is. 43:25).

Second is the glorious truth of **God's Fatherhood** and His promises to His children. We are assured: 'even the very hairs of your head are all numbered' (Matt. 10:30). David understood this well: 'My flesh and my heart may fail, but God is the strength of my heart and my portion for ever' (Ps. 73:26). Yet the enemy of souls endeavours to rob us of such assurances.

Third is our wonderful hope of **heaven**. While our old age prompts occasional or even frequent groans, never forget what should accompany them: our longing for heaven (2 Cor. 5:1–5). In old age the body becomes like an old car to which we may be very attached. But there comes a time, no matter how well serviced it may be, when some things go wrong – at first small concerns and then larger. The benefit of this is that it makes us long even more for the model that will never go wrong – our resurrection bodies (1 Cor. 15:35–58)!

A spiritual priority for old age!

In addition to remembering these key truths, we would be wise to **focus our thoughts daily upon our Lord Jesus Christ**. Remember He is the Father's delight, and He should be ours too. He 'is the same yesterday and today and for ever' (Heb. 13:8). The enemy of souls will try to distract us from this essential exercise of faith for he knows that it will unfailingly deliver us from spiritual dangers. Meditate especially upon the cross and all that our Saviour accomplished there so that you never lose your sense of infinite indebtedness to Him.

Practical priorities in old age

With these spiritual realities firmly in mind, it is nevertheless right to take into account practical considerations:

Delegation. It is a stage of life to hand over your responsibilities while you are still able to do so competently and can offer initial support to those taking charge.

Down-sizing. This, should it be necessary, has to be done while we are fit enough to cope with it, otherwise we will leave it too late.

Setting our affairs in order. It is right to give this consideration (see Is. 38:1). Give a trusted person or persons – ideally a member or members of your family – the power of attorney. To do it now may prove more important than you anticipate. Make sure you have made your will and that it is up to date. Write down your wishes for the funeral and thanksgiving service at your death. It may be helpful to leave a note as to whom you would like to have your personal treasures. But whatever you do, do not worry about your assets when you die. Your best possessions as a Christian have already gone before you!

A PRAYER

Heavenly Father, whatever may be happening to me because of my increasing age, help me to forget the things behind me that I ought to forget and instead strain towards what is ahead, pressing on towards the goal to win the prize for which You have called me heavenwards in Christ Jesus. For His Name's sake. Amen.

A IS FOR ACCEPTANCE

Barzillai proved himself a special friend of David. He provided shelter and safety for him (2 Sam. 17:27–29) when David's third son, Absalom, initiated a rebellion against his rule. David wept at the news of his rebellious son's death. But this also meant David no longer needed Barzillai's protective hospitality. What would happen next?

Let's take up the story:

Now Barzillai was a very old man, eighty years of age. He had provided for the king during his stay … for he was a very wealthy man. The king said to Barzillai, 'Cross over with me and stay with me in Jerusalem, and I will provide for you.'

But Barzillai answered the king, 'How many more years shall I live, that I should go up to Jerusalem with the king? I am now eighty years old. Can I tell the difference between what is good and what is not? Can your servant taste what he eats and drinks? Can I still hear the voices of men and women singers? Why should your servant be an added burden to my lord the king? Your servant will cross over the Jordan with the king for a short distance, but why should the king reward me in this way? Let your servant return, that I may die in my own town near the tomb of my father and mother' (2 Sam. 19:32–37).

This passage shows us six truths Barzillai accepted because of his age:

1. His wealth was no protection against old age (v. 32).
2. His evaluation about what was enjoyable and what was not was now uncertain (v. 35).
3. His sense of taste had gone (v. 35).
4. His hearing was not what it had been (v. 35).
5. His travelling days were done (v. 37).
6. He did not want his age to be a burden to others (v. 35).

Post the flood, 'three score years and ten' is a

reasonable time to live. Our bodies don't live as long since the flood no matter what the wonders of medical science may achieve. 'The length of our days is seventy years – or eighty, if we have the strength; yet their span is but trouble and sorrow, for they quickly pass, and we fly away' (Ps. 90:10), and often they finish 'with a moan' (Ps. 90:9).

Accepting the onset of old age

A key attitude towards the onset of old age is therefore acceptance that this is a natural part of human life. We need to accept it in all its facets.

Accept the inescapable indignities and embarrassments of old age

I remember how I suddenly felt embarrassingly old when a young doctor, whom I had not met before, put me on a weekly appointment for six weeks at an assessment clinic in an Edinburgh hospital geared to the care of the elderly.

Accept the gradual loss of independence in some areas of life

Most of us are naturally independent. For example, it is hard to give up our driving licence, making us dependent on lifts by our friends with cars. Inevitably we have to accept practical help and support, especially from our family and friends. I never want to be a burden to my family and friends and I strive after independence. But I have now learned to accept that one day I may be dependent upon them, if only for them to be the best judge in deciding what kind of care I may need, a decision I may then be incapable of making myself. I would much prefer that the Lord would bring forward my 'exodus' or departure from this life before that time, but that is in His hands alone.

Accept that increasing age brings more frustrations
Chief of these are tiredness, limited energy and the length of time it takes to do things that we once did quickly. We also find it difficult to think of going away for a holiday. Like Moses, who at a great age was contemplating travel, we are 'no longer able' as once we were (Deut. 31:2). But acceptance means looking back, remembering our enjoyment of our holidays and energetic enjoyments, and spending time thanking God for them. Why not take time today to take out those old photos or look at those mementos you treasure to stir your mind with thankfulness?

I am slowly learning to give myself 'a good talking to'! Thank God that it is only in later life I have known such frustrations. My level of experiencing them is an indication of how much I have been able to do in the past, not realising how blessed I have been. We need to beware of negativity if we are to be genuinely accepting of our circumstances and needs.

We must also not be surprised that younger people may not understand the frustrations and physical challenges old age presents. Looking back, I recognise my own lack of understanding of old age, especially of the loneliness it may bring.

If we have children, they may vary in their attentiveness or sensitivity towards us. But pause for a moment and remember how busy you were at their age and perhaps your own insensitivity to your parents or elderly folk. The same is true of those in our church fellowship or in the social and medical services.

Accepting the changing of times

This is perhaps the greatest test of acceptance we face. Do we honestly take on board the truth that times change and that it is unhelpful to talk of the past as 'the good old days'? Not only has society changed with the development of technology, but church life has changed. We sing different hymns and songs, while some old ones we love are now unknown. Instead of using a hymn book, we may sing from a screen. The organ may be replaced by a band. I find myself wanting to wear a tie to church although it is no longer the norm.

When I begin to hang on to such things so that I begrudge their absence, I must say to myself, 'Beware.' Sadly church fellowships may be torn apart through the non-acceptance of change, and tragically the older generation may be cut off from the rising generation.

If you will allow me, providing you are old enough, I want to invite you to free membership of the Barzillai Club!

PRAYERS FOR
A MORE ACCEPTING ATTITUDE

Lord, enable me to accept that all my circumstances are ordained by You for my good.

O Lord Jesus Christ, who has created and redeemed me, You know what You would do with me. Do with me, according to Your will, for Your mercy's sake. Amen (King Henry IV).

B IS FOR BELIEVE

Belief and faith are almost interchangeable words, and it makes sense to deal with them together. *Belief* is about truths of which we are persuaded or confident. *Faith* goes further because it implies action, putting what we believe into practice.

It is first important to know what we believe. I believe the books of the Bible share a common inspiration from God the Holy Spirit, and that they contain everything I am to believe and do so that my soul may be saved and God served. The Old Testament gives the first promise of a Saviour in the book of Genesis, with further details of this unfolding through the prophets. The New Testament reveals how that promise has been fulfilled in Jesus' incarnation, His unique atoning death for our sins, His resurrection from the dead, His ascension to heaven and the promise of His second coming. The Bible's essential message is: 'Believe in the Lord Jesus, and you will be saved' (Acts 16:31).

Believing this message requires actions of faith. We are to repent of our sins, understanding how Jesus in His death on the cross stood in the place of sinners. He took upon Himself the punishment we deserve that we might be put right with God. We are to confess then with our mouth *what* we have believed in our heart (Rom. 10:8–10).

As important as knowing what we believe is knowing *whom* we have believed (2 Tim. 1:12). A subtle way the enemy of souls tempts us in old age to doubt what we believe is when he encourages us to forget in whom we have believed. That belief, genuinely held, changes our lives. It turned Paul, the persecutor of first-century believers, into the determined and unashamed preacher of the cross: 'May I never boast except in the cross of our Lord Jesus Christ' (Gal. 6:14).

Paul and the other apostles knew that in this human life they would never attain perfection and perfect likeness to their Saviour. Yet they also knew that as we daily confess our sins, God 'is faithful and just and will forgive us our sins' (1 John 1:9). Do not be surprised that your sense of sin increases in old age.

How exactly do our beliefs work out in our faith and life?

The most telling description of belief turned into active faith is Hebrews 11, where we learn from the example of others the following.

Faith prompts us to offer only our best to God (Abel, v. 4)

Our most valuable assets in old age are time to pray and resources to share and give away.

Faith causes us to reckon walking with God the most important thing in life (Enoch, v. 5)

The times we spend daily in fellowship with God, praying and reading His Word, can be the most precious times, particularly as they lead to daily obedience.

Faith makes us concerned for the saving of our household (Noah, v. 7)

We all belong to human families, and it is likely within them are those for whose spiritual well-being we daily pray. Some prayers may only be answered after we have died.

Faith helps us to obey God, even blindly sometimes, when we do not know where that obedience may lead us (Abraham, v. 8)

Decision-making does not become easier as we get older. Praying about our decisions may often pleasantly surprise us as we then hear God's voice through the advice we receive from those whom we trust.

Faith shows us how we should live our lives like refugees in the world, holding lightly to our human possessions (Abraham and his immediate descendants, vv. 9–10, 13–16)

I want to live as someone who knows that my real treasures are in heaven.

Faith changes our minds about things once thought impossible (Sarah, vv. 11–12)

It is encouraging that Sarah is included in this list because she had to be brought from a position of unbelief to faith.

Faith enables us to obey God implicitly no matter what the cost (Abraham, seen in his offering Isaac, vv. 17–19)

Faith may be responding to a costly or demanding

need we are able to meet. It enables us to obey and to know peace and joy in doing so.

Faith makes us concerned for the spiritual well-being of the coming generations of our family (Isaac, seen in his blessing Jacob and Esau, v. 20)
Believing prayer should mark our prayer for those related to us and those yet unborn.

Faith, wonderfully, gives us confidence in the face of death (Jacob and Joseph, vv. 21–22)
Like David we may say, 'My times are in your hands' (Ps. 31:15).

Faith enables us to co-operate actively with God's purposes by doing our best, even though we may not realise how important that co-operation may be (Moses' parents, v. 23)
Moses' parents could not have guessed how significant their actions were, but they certainly acted in faith.

Faith drives away fear as it fixes its eyes upon God, invisible as He is (Moses, before Pharaoh, v. 27)
Every time I am afraid I know the answer is to look up to my Heavenly Father and trust Him for His peace and help.

Faith brings success and victory against all odds (the amazing fall of the city of Jericho, v. 30)

We all have our 'Jerichos' and some of them are peculiar to old age. Every 'Jericho' can be overcome as we exercise faith.

A PRAYER FOR BELIEF

Lord, please forgive my unbelief when faced with the growing difficulties and challenges of old age. Thank You for Your unchanging character as my Heavenly Father and for my Saviour who is the same yesterday, today and forever. Help me to fix my eyes upon Him as I face my 'Jerichos'. May I so live a life of faith that I leave a good testimony to all my family and friends when You call me home. I ask this in the Name of the Lord Jesus. Amen.

C IS FOR CONTENTMENT

Some of us are more content by nature than others. This may be influenced by our temperament, childhood and the parents to whom we were born and their unconscious example.

Areas of life may bring both contentment and discontent. The first sphere this is seen in is clearly **our family and friends**. We can be proud of them, but it may be that we see all too little of them, perhaps making us think they do not care much about us. Rather than thanking God for them and all that they do for us from time to time, we are disappointed in them.

The second area is **our health**. Old age brings health problems, more to some than others. Perhaps in the past we scarcely ever thanked God for the health we enjoyed. But now our diary records many visits to doctors and hospital clinics. Preoccupation with physical ailments or disability may almost blind us to the benefits we daily enjoy.

The third area may be **our finances**. It is so easy to look enviously at those who are better off, so that we fail to commiserate with and to be concerned for those who are worse off than we are. A problem as we get older may be that because our expenditure is small compared with what it used to be, we accumulate money, and we are at a loss as to how to use it wisely for the benefit of the members of our family and others.

The fourth area may be discontent with **our circumstances**. Perhaps when our family members come to see us, their visits seem all too short. If we have carers, we may be discontented with the haste with which they do everything.

A priority – and a great secret

The key to contentment is understanding and living according to the priority of the health of our soul (Mark 8:36). In the Book of Psalms we find the writer talking to his soul: 'Why are you downcast, O my soul? Why so disturbed within me? Put your hope in God, for I will yet praise him, my Saviour and my God' (Ps. 43:5).

The apostle Paul shares how he too had learned the secret of being content. When the Philippian believers heard that he had been put into a Roman prison yet again, they were concerned for him. They knew that he would have many practical needs, but they could not do a bank transfer of funds as we may do today. The answer was sending gifts with Epaphroditus, a church member. But it was not a glum, self-pitying man he found. One word summed up Paul's state: contentment!

Paul's letter to the Philippians – the Christians living in Philippi, where he had seen the first church in Europe established – is a 'thank you' letter:

I rejoice greatly in the Lord that at last you have renewed your concern for me. Indeed, you have been concerned, but you had no opportunity to show it. I am not saying this because I am in need, for I have learned the secret to be content whatever the circumstances. *I know what it is to be in need, and what it is to have plenty. I have learned* the secret *of being content in any and every situation, whether well fed or hungry, whether living in plenty or in want (Phil. 4:10–12,* my emphasis*).*

The explanation for Paul's attitude is found in the next verse: 'I can do everything through him who gives me strength' (v. 13). This was a truth built into Paul's Christian experience. Contentment increases when we recognise that God is in control of our circumstances and that, wherever we are, God's purpose is to bring into our lives people who need our Saviour. Contentment may be a telltale witness to them of the reality of our faith.

I want to avoid any kind of glibness in writing in this way, but I am encouraged by the telling word that Paul uses twice in Philippians 4:10–13 – it is the word 'learned'. **Contentment is something we have to learn.** But more than that, **we have to keep on learning it in the twist and turns of our life!** Paul's secret can be ours! Having the Lord Jesus as my Saviour and Lord, I have everything I need, together with a most glorious eternal future! This truth is like a comfortable pillow upon which to rest, calculated to help my contentment whatever my circumstances. That does not mean that the enemy of souls may not try to undermine my contentment; he will attempt to do so because he knows how vital it is to my testimony to my Saviour's grace and help.

Day by day the reading of the Scriptures feeds our contentment. Our contentment is not only a blessing to us but an unconscious witness to others of what it means to belong to the Lord Jesus. There is nothing worse than a grumpy old man or woman! I wonder how people think of us?

A PRAYER FOR CONTENTMENT IN OLD AGE

Father, You know the challenges I face and my disappointment in myself when I do not respond to them as I ought. Thank You that You are my Father, the Lord Jesus is my Saviour, and the Holy Spirit is my indwelling Friend and Guide. Please keep my eyes open to my spiritual riches and may my life witness, without my realising it, what it means to be satisfied in knowing You. In Jesus' Name I pray. Amen.

D IS FOR DISCIPLESHIP

What prompted me to choose discipleship for the letter 'D' was reading Luke's description of Mnason, a first-century Cyprian Christian, as 'one of the early disciples' or 'an old disciple' (Acts 21:16, KJV). Although old, perhaps converted on the Day of Pentecost, Mnason had stayed the course, and was still running the race of discipleship in the final stages of his earthly life.

Come, follow!

It was the simplest of invitations, but one of profound significance to the first followers of Jesus. Two brothers, Peter and Andrew, were about to cast a net into the sea when the Lord Jesus said to them, 'Come, follow me ... and I will make you fishers of men' (Matt. 4:19). It is good to remember that moment when we first heard Jesus' call and put our trust in Him.

We did not realise then all that the life of discipleship was going to mean, and perhaps the cost it would sometimes involve, as the years passed. This was the case for Peter and Andrew. But any journey begins with the first step.

Their next step was to *listen to Him daily* and to *obey Him*. So it is with us. Obeying Him we become like the wise man who built his house upon a rock (Luke 6:46–49). We cannot genuinely call Jesus 'Lord' without doing what He teaches. The more we listen to the Lord Jesus and obey Him, the more we become like Him: 'A student is not above his teacher, but everyone who is fully trained will be like his teacher' (Luke 6:40).

Jesus never underplayed the challenge, difficulties and personal suffering discipleship may bring: 'No-one who puts his hand to the plough and looks back is fit for service in the kingdom of God' (Luke 9:62). But disciples are expected to *make a difference* simply by being like their Lord and Master. Wherever we are, wherever we live, we are to be like salt and light. In that way we may often surprise people with the kind of actions and behaviour our Saviour exemplified – even washing people's feet. Jesus' words are not past but present tense: 'Now that you know these things, you will be blessed if you do them' (John 13:17).

Peter learnt this lesson well and then passed it on: 'For it is commendable if a man bears up under the pain of unjust suffering because he is conscious of God … To this you were called, because Christ suffered for you, leaving you an example, *that you should follow in his steps*' (1 Pet. 2:19, 21, my italics). Those four words – 'follow in his steps' – are fundamental to understanding what it means to be a disciple.

The apostle Paul accepted the challenge of discipleship and rejoiced in the fellowship of Christ's sufferings. He grieved over the lost and sought them earnestly. He was willing to go to any lengths to identify with Christ in His sufferings in order to win some. As a fisher of men and women, he cast out the gospel net every time he preached publicly or spoke to individuals.

Follow Jesus to your dying days

Our Lord Jesus' call to discipleship is as real and relevant in old age as at any age through which we have passed. We probably see and talk more to older folk than younger, but they all need the only Saviour, our Lord Jesus Christ. Just where God has placed you now, where you are reading these words, God has put you to be a witness to His Son and His cross. We are to confess unashamedly our faith in Him.

A good question to ask ourselves, therefore, is: are we known as Christians? Is it obvious that we are on the side of Jesus Christ? Is it plain that we seek to please Him before anyone else? If we can honestly respond 'yes', then this is true Christian discipleship. Moreover, we have an important reason for our Christian testimony to Jesus: 'For here we do not have an enduring city, but we are looking for the city which is to come' (Heb. 13:14). We know that our Saviour has gone to prepare a place for us, but many all around us do not have that hope and assurance. We may be the only people they know who are able to explain how they may possess it too.

Be a disciplined disciple

There is a relationship between the word 'discipleship' and the word 'discipline'. Paul urged Timothy, 'Endure hardship with us like a good soldier of Christ Jesus' (2 Tim. 2:3). If there is one quality that marks a good soldier it is discipline.

We need to be disciplined in three areas in particular: in prayer, Bible reading and the use of time. In old age it is all too easy to be off our guard against a sharp attack of Satan, the enemy of souls, but we mustn't be neglectful.

Why is discipleship so important in old age?

- Discipleship is a lifetime calling and privilege.
- Every stage of life brings new discipleship challenges, opportunities and experiences.
- Discipleship carries the responsibility for passing on to the next generation all we have learnt and gained.
- Our lives have the potential for being the best textbook on discipleship for our children, grandchildren and great-grandchildren.
- Daily discipleship will help us not to be grumpy old men and women.

A PRAYER FOR FAITHFUL DISCIPLESHIP

Almighty God, the God and Father of our Lord Jesus, I thank You for that time in my life when I first heard Your Son's call to follow Him. Thank You for the human instruments You used and their example of discipleship. Grant that where I am now, whatever my physical limitations, I may be eager to share the Saviour's call to others, and that although old I might be known supremely as an aged disciple, like Mnason. I ask this not for my own satisfaction, but for the sake of Him who died and rose again for me. Amen.

E IS FOR ENCOURAGE

An outstanding example of an encourager is Barnabas. That was not his birth name. The apostles changed his name from Joseph to Barnabas because the latter's meaning is 'son of encouragement'. What a tribute! When, for example, at the time of Paul's conversion, many Christians were afraid of him, not believing that he was really a disciple, Barnabas took him to the apostles so that they might hear his testimony (Acts 9:26–27). Later he introduced Paul to the church at Antioch and together they taught the people – the first to be called 'Christians' – there (Acts 11:25–26).

Significantly, Paul himself then became a great encourager, no doubt inspired by Barnabas' example. Every letter of Paul's found in the New Testament is one of encouragement. He identified encouragement as a spiritual gift given to the body of Christ, the Church (Rom. 12:8; 1 Cor. 14:3–4).

Spheres of encouragement

There are many areas in which we can encourage others.

Our church family

The first area for encouragement is the church family to which we belong. We should begin with those who are in spiritual leadership because, while a vital part of the work of pastors and teachers is to encourage, they also need to be encouraged. Aim never to be an unhelpful critic of what is going on in the life of God's people, but be an encourager. Remember: 'An anxious heart weighs a man down, but a kind word cheers him up' (Prov. 12:25).

Our generation

Another sphere for encouragement is among the people of our own generation, our fellow 'oldies'. I go to a seniors' monthly lunch. We are picked up by car and brought back home afterwards. I don't choose who the other passengers are and I don't know with whom I will sit around a table for lunch, but God does. I realise that one of His purposes is *always* that I may encourage such individuals.

Likewise, every month we have a coffee morning for the thirty flats where I live. Once, seeing one of the residents sitting on her own, I went and sat next to her, rather than sitting with those whom I know well. I asked her about her family and interests. At the end, to my surprise, she said, 'Thank you so much for coming to talk to me.'

Young people

Equally we can help and influence the young people we may meet at church. When I was brought to faith in the Lord Jesus in my teens, having not come from a Christian background, the most significant encouragers for me were old people. One regularly gave me helpful books to read, encouraging my appetite for reading Christian literature. After the first church prayer meeting I went to, at the age of fifteen, the lady next to whom I sat turned to me and said, 'Why didn't you pray?' That encouraged me to never again go without participating! When I did my National Service, an elderly man wrote down notes of our minister's Sunday sermons and posted them on Monday so that without fail I received them on Tuesday.

Letters, phone calls and emails are all vehicles of encouragement. Not all of us are at home with contemporary technology, but most of us can write letters or make phone calls. Why not reserve one evening a week for people you know who will be encouraged by a phone call and a prayer together?

Simple actions encourage

If the thought comes to you of someone who may be lonely or discouraged, who might appreciate a phone call, or a letter, or an invitation to come and have a tea or coffee, do it! Who do you know who is inclined to be timid and discouraged? Follow the Bible's guidance and 'encourage the timid, help the weak, be patient with everyone' (1 Thes. 5:14).

In our old age we will find ourselves seeing many friends and acquaintances bereaved. Then is the time to tenderly and graciously remind them and ourselves of our living hope and glorious assurance of eternal life and a place in the Father's house. Our encouragement will be all the greater if we ourselves have passed along the same path of bereavement.

Sometimes it may be that such an individual is one you do not know well, but you know something of his or her needs. This happened once among the

Christians in Rome. They heard that the authorities were transporting the apostle Paul to Rome to be put on trial. Some of them took time off work and travelled to one of Paul's stopping points on his journey. He had never seen them before but 'at the sight of these men Paul thanked God and was encouraged' (Acts 28:15).

At other times we may need to adapt our methods. As I get older I am not physically able to visit people, yet many of them are physically able to visit me – if I invite them. I can't easily cook them a meal, but I can put the kettle on.

Everyone – great or small – needs encouragement at times in life, but, sadly, some are never or seldom given it. Carers too need encouragement as well as those who receive care from them. Even the strongest Christians we know needs timely encouragement.

Finally, do not forget to encourage yourself by the Scriptures. David's testimony can be ours: 'I sought the LORD, and he answered me; he delivered me from all my fears. Those who look to him are radiant' (Ps. 34:4–5).

Why is giving encouragement so important in old age?

- It is a stage in life when we are most in need of it and are also best able to give it to others through our long experience of God's goodness.
- The more we give encouragement, the more we are encouraged.
- It is a worthy ambition to leave behind the memory of being a Barnabas and not a grumbler or discourager!

I wonder if people think of us as a 'Barnabas'?

A PRAYER TO BE AN ENCOURAGER

Heavenly Father, help me to be like Barnabas. Forgive me when I have been more concerned to receive encouragement than to give it. Make me sensitive to the needs of people around me so that I may bring them Your encouragement. I ask this in Jesus' Name. Amen.

F IS FOR
THE FEAR OF GOD

Old age brings many fears. Common fears are the prospect of our mind failing us; becoming forgetful; losing our independence or our sight and hearing; or being a burden to our family. A financial fear may be of our inability to obtain and sustain the care we may need. Then there is the fear of loneliness or of simply not being able to cope with life. You will be able to add to the list. I hope that I am not depressing you!

David's key understanding

I love Psalm 34 because it provides us with the answer to all our fears, at whatever age we have arrived, in the context of fearing God. Let me list some of the fears it mentions:

- Afflictions that take the joy out of life (v. 2).
- Having not just one fear but many (v. 4).

- Troubles that make us long for help (vv. 6, 17).
- Areas of need in our life, perhaps financial or physical, that expose our vulnerability to fear (vv. 9–10).
- Being broken-hearted, depressed, distressed (v. 18) and surrounded by troubles (v. 19).

It is quite a list! And yet it is a wonderfully joyful psalm giving praise and thanks to God! Reading it we have to ask, what's the explanation for this joy? The secret is that David knew the reality of the fear of God in his life and he testifies to the fact: 'The angel of the LORD encamps around those who fear him, and he delivers them. Taste and see that the LORD is good; blessed is the man who takes refuge in him. Fear the LORD, you his saints, for those who fear him lack nothing' (vv. 7–9). David was so confident of this secret that he wanted to pass it on to all his family: 'Come, my children, listen to me; I will teach you the fear of the LORD' (v. 11).

The way God keeps His promises

When God-fearing men and women in the Old Testament period became aware of their sin, they offered the sacrifices God had prescribed. While these could never take away sin, they looked forward to that being achieved by the unique sacrifice of the Lord Jesus upon the cross.

Wonderfully and gloriously the New Testament shows God fulfilling His promise, made in the Garden of Eden, of a Saviour of sinners. Thus we enjoy this glorious consequence: 'you did not receive a spirit that makes you a slave again to fear, but you received the Spirit of sonship. And by him we cry, "*Abba*, Father"' (Rom. 8:15). At our new birth God becomes *our* Father! The picture we should then have in our mind of God becomes that of the father in the story the Lord Jesus told of the prodigal son. God has rushed out to welcome us, He has clothed us in the righteousness of His Son, our Saviour, and has made us members of His family. Slavish or unworthy dread of God is displaced by a delight in loving and pleasing Him. We discover that 'the fear of the LORD is the beginning of wisdom, and knowledge of the Holy One is understanding' (Prov. 9:10).

Defining the fear of the Lord

The enemy of souls wants us to think that the fear of the Lord is unimportant. He hates our living in a rightful respect and honouring of God. He will whisper, 'How can you believe God's love for you if you have to fear Him?' We need to remember what our Lord Jesus said of the devil: 'there is no truth in him. When he lies, he speaks his native language, for he is a liar and the father of lies' (John 8:44).

If you and I had a good human father – and, regretfully, not everyone has had that experience – we will have revered and respected him, perhaps even more now than when we were young. He will have had to discipline us on many occasions, but we would never have doubted his love for us. In fact, his discipline was part of his love for us, as was our mother's. We would not have wanted anyone to show disrespect for our father so we would have stuck up for his name and been proud of our relationship to him.

This is even more so with regard to our knowing God as our Father. Our first request in the Lord's Prayer is: 'hallowed be your name' (Matt. 6:9). This highlights what the fear of God means: it is to respect greatly all that God has revealed of His character so that we live our lives honouring Him, the perfect Father, and aiming to have Him in His right place in every part of our life.

Unconsciously almost, David's Psalm 34 reveals the benefits and consequences of this:

- We want to extol and bless the Lord at all times (v. 1).
- His praise is always on our lips (v. 1).
- Our soul boasts in the Lord so that we bring encouragement and joy to those whom we know who are afflicted in some way (v. 2)
- We glorify and exalt the Lord and delight to do so with others who fear Him (v. 3).
- We seek the Lord in prayer and know Him answering our prayers (vv. 4, 6, 17).
- We look to Him and are made radiant for He never disappoints us (v. 5).
- We daily prove God's goodness and strength (v. 8).
- We discover that fearing Him we have nothing else to fear (v. 9)!

Why is the fear of the Lord so important in old age?
To teach the fear of the Lord and to display its beauty to all who are closest to us is the greatest service we can do for them: 'Come, my children, listen to me; I will teach you the fear of the LORD' (Ps. 34:11).

A PRAYER FOR A LIFE THAT FEARS GOD

Heavenly Father, help me so to know and love You that, unconsciously, I may display the wisdom, attractiveness and beauty of a life that fears and delights in knowing You. For Jesus' sake. Amen.

G IS FOR GODLINESS

Nothing could be more appropriate than for 'F ... for the *fear of God*' to be followed by 'G ... for *godliness*' since the latter is the consequence of the former. What will we leave to our family? What will be their inheritance? The best benefit we can leave is the remembrance of a godly life!

Old age is a time when we have to give up things. We cannot do as once we did things that require lots of physical energy, like running or jumping. Even walking may be limited and sometimes a problem. We have to give up holding positions of responsibility in the community or in our church fellowship. We have to let go and not hold on to things that ought to be given up. But there is one thing we can do until our dying days: we can pursue godliness (1 Tim. 6:11).

Godliness sounds as old-fashioned as the fear of God, but they go hand in hand in both in the

Old and New Testaments. Their irreplaceability demands that we reinstate their importance. In the New Testament the word for godliness is made up of two parts: the adverb meaning 'well' and the verb 'to be devout'. This provides its best explanation: godliness is being and doing what God requires of us in a way that is 'well' pleasing to Him. Or, better still, **godliness is doing what is right in every part of our life with an eye to God's approval alone**.

The Lord Jesus' instruction

Our Saviour's teaching in the Sermon of the Mount illustrates this definition of godliness, particularly in these three areas.

Giving

First, regarding giving, the Lord Jesus warns,

> *Be careful not to do your 'acts of righteousness' before men, to be seen by them. If you do, you will have no reward from your Father in heaven.*

> *So when you give to the needy, do not announce it with trumpets, as the hypocrites do in the synagogues and on the streets, to be honoured by*

men ... But when you give to the needy, do not let your left hand know what your right hand is doing, so that your giving may be in secret. Then your Father, who sees what is done in secret, will reward you (Matt. 6:1–4).

Some charities give donors the opportunity to have their names published in their magazine or, if they wish, to remain anonymous. Which would we choose?

Prayer

Second, the Lord Jesus speaks about prayer in a similar way:

And when you pray, do not be like the hypocrites, for they love to pray standing in the synagogues and on the street corners to be seen of men ... But when you pray, go into your room, close the door and pray to your Father, who is unseen. Then your Father, who sees what is done in secret, will reward you (Matt. 6:5–6).

It is good to pray together with other Christians, but not in order to be admired for our eloquence or spirituality.

Fasting

The third illustration the Lord Jesus gives concerns fasting:

> *When you fast, do not look sombre as the hypocrites do, for they disfigure their faces to show men they are fasting ... But when you fast, put oil on your head and wash your face, so that it will not be obvious to men that you are fasting, but only to your Father, who is unseen; and your Father, who sees what is done in secret, will reward you (Matt. 6:16–18).*

Fasting is not going around looking miserable and hungry, prompting people to ask, 'Why are you looking so much out of sorts and glum?' Answering that question might sadly express our pride and personal ego to the detriment of the development of genuine godliness in our lives.

All three examples – giving, praying and fasting – underline that godliness is doing what we know pleases God with our eyes on His approval alone.

The Lord Jesus' ultimate example

The supreme example of godliness is our Lord Jesus Christ. This is one among many reasons why we are regularly urged in the New Testament to fix our eyes upon Him. Twice in the gospels God the Father declares, 'This is my Son, whom I love; with him I am well pleased' (Matt. 3:17; 17:5).

The godliness of the Lord Jesus meant that whether in public or secret He delighted to do His Father's will, aiming always to please Him above all others (Heb. 10:5–7). Godly men and women do not live according to the world's standards, but those of God. His commandments are their delight and they are unashamed in their obedience to them.

The achievement of godliness

We need to identify spiritual priorities and then pursue them. This requires not only God's power but effort and practice on our part like an athlete striving after the best (2 Pet. 1:3, 5).

Once, I went to two local gyms to look at their facilities. When I saw the range of equipment and the energy required, I realised that such activity was beyond me! But old age does not interfere with my being a spiritual gymnast (2 Pet. 1:5–9)!

So, as you read the Bible, ask yourself, what is God calling me to be and do? Remember that it is 'the knowledge of the truth that leads to godliness'

(Tit. 1:1). Godliness is possible only as our conscience is exposed and brought into obedience to God. To this end it helps to have a notebook by you when you read the Bible to write down truths that you need to ponder and respond to as you pray.

Why is godliness so important in old age?

- Godliness brings God's blessing and true happiness (Ps. 1:1–3).
- It is the evidence of mature spiritual fruit in our lives that glorifies God.
- It holds the promise of godly offspring (Mal. 2:15).
- It is the best inheritance we can leave our family and friends.

A PRAYER FOR THE PURSUIT OF GODLINESS

Teach me, my God and King,
In all things Thee to see,
And what I do in anything
To do it as for Thee.

(George Herbert)[1]

H IS FOR HOPE

Hope is not a word commonly associated with old age. I have no hope of looking younger, of being a squash or tennis player, and now even of driving a car! When the TV shows old people in a care home, few if any may be mobile or even awake. However, as a Christian I do have hope, a hope that burns more brightly the older I get.

We live in a world marked by hopelessness. The greatest issue is death's reality, whether we are wealthy or poor, physically well or ill. In the face of death the great majority of people are without hope. They do not want to talk about it. We have only to go to a secular funeral to have our eyes opened to the harsh reality of life without hope.

Christian hope

The understanding of the biblical word 'hope' is different from the common use in daily speech. When we speak of the weather prospects, we say we hope it will not rain, knowing that we cannot speak with any certainty about it. We take an umbrella with us in case we need it! We hope that a new government will work wonders where there has been conspicuous failure in the past, but it may prove to be wishful thinking.

I can remember the anticipation of one of my sons, many years ago, as we approached his birthday. He had expressed his wish for a camera and we had promised him such. My wife and I bought the camera and carefully placed it on top of a wardrobe in our bedroom where it could not be seen, ready to be produced on the required day. Days before his birthday I overheard him say to one of his school friends, 'I *have* a camera for my birthday.' He was perfectly correct, although he had not seen it, because he was certain of the integrity of those who had promised it to him, although perhaps unaware of how far it would exceed his expectations.

We may be perfectly certain of the integrity of the One who promises eternal life to us through His Son: 'God is not a man, that he should lie' (Num. 23:19). Therefore we can be sure of all the following:

- Our Lord Jesus, by His death and resurrection, has conquered death for all who put their trust in Him.
- For Christians, therefore, to die is to be forever with the Lord. Their bodies fall asleep, awaiting the day of resurrection, and, meanwhile, their spirits are consciously with their Saviour.
- The realisation of this hope will be far more wonderful than our limited minds and understanding can ever anticipate (1 Cor. 2:9).
- It is 'hope of the glory of God' (Rom. 5:2). 'Glory' is the radiant brightness of God's presence, a word that is also used to describe the glory of all that God is.
- We are to share in His glory. God's good work in us is to conform us into the likeness of His Son (Rom. 8:29; Phil. 1:6) and will reach its glorious completion at our Saviour's return (1 John 3:2).
- Already 'our citizenship is in heaven. And we eagerly await a Saviour from there, the Lord Jesus Christ, who, by the power that enables him to bring everything under his control, will transform our lowly bodies so that they will be like his glorious body' (Phil. 3:20–21).

- The difficulties of old age do not need to diminish our hope; rather, they may enrich it and make our anticipation of it all the more real (Rom. 5:2–4).
- It is a hope that will not disappoint us and is made all the more certain because of our sure knowledge of the love of the One who promises it to us (Rom. 5:5).
- It is a hope that enables us to rejoice whatever our troubles, tragedies and difficulties (Rom. 15:4).
- Hope – of our sure salvation – is like a helmet (Eph. 6:17) that we need to put on when the enemy of souls endeavours to sow doubts in our minds, something he especially does when troubles, illnesses and tragedies occur in our lives.

Why is hope so important in old age?

- My hope's realisation is closer now than when I first believed.
- In old age I am in 'the departure lounge', waiting for God's call home!
- Every day I meet people who have no

hope and I may be the only person with the opportunity to share this good news with them.

- The evidences in my life that I have hope will prompt people to ask me the reason for the hope that I have.
- Hope means that in old age rather than thinking always wistfully about the past and what I am missing, I will be thinking with eager anticipation of what God promises me in the future through His Son's saving work.
- Hope means that when we attend the funeral of someone we love, we can both smile and shed a tear at one and the same time. The Bible calls it holding 'on to our courage and the hope of which we boast' (Heb. 3:6).

A PRAYER FOR UNWAVERING HOPE

Our Heavenly Father, we rejoice to own You as the God of hope. Please fill us with all joy and peace as we trust in You, so that we may overflow with hope by the power of the Holy Spirit. May we be able to sing:

My hope is built on nothing less
Than Jesus' blood and righteousness;

I dare not trust the sweetest frame,
But wholly lean on Jesus' name.

On Christ, the solid Rock, I stand;
All other ground is sinking sand.

(Edward Mote)[2]

and

Keep us, Lord, O keep us cleaving
To Thyself, and still believing,
Till the hour of our receiving
Promised joys with Thee.

Then we shall be where we would be,
Then we shall be what we should be;
Things that are not now, nor could be,
Soon shall be our own.

(Thomas Kelly)[3]

We pray in Jesus' Name. Amen.

I IS FOR
INTERCESSION

Prayer has different parts, all of which are important, but none more than intercession. It has special relevance in old age. As we get older, we inevitably forego active participation in many church activities, but we are able to set aside time for intercession. Old people can be key intercessors in any church fellowship.

Our long experience of life means that we are able to pray with understanding for the tasks we once did which others now fulfil. As grandparents and great-grandparents, we can pray for the challenges our children and grandchildren face in the upbringing of their children. Our age also inevitably brings the experience of bereavement and we are equipped, therefore, to pray with understanding for those who are bereaved. Yet we are not just to pray for those who are close to us.

Intercession should be made for everyone

Paul wrote,

> *I urge, then, first of all, that requests, prayers, intercession and thanksgiving be made for everyone – for kings and all those in authority, that we may live peaceful and quiet lives in all godliness and holiness. This is good, and pleases God our Saviour, who wants all men to be saved and to come to a knowledge of the truth (1 Tim. 2:1–4).*

As God's concern is for all men and women the world over, so too must ours. **Governments and rulers** are not to be neglected in our intercession. There will not be a single day when on the radio or television news matters don't arise that should prompt us to pray, whether it be matters of government policy or the urgent needs of refugees or people being overwhelmed by natural disasters. Why not listen to every news bulletin with a view to making its **urgent issues** an immediate matter for prayer? Similarly, every time I hear an ambulance or police siren I feel it appropriate to pray for those in danger and those going to assist them. I am ignorant of the details, but God is not.

Intercession should also be made for **those who hold special responsibilities of spiritual leadership**. Sometimes decisions or ways of doing things may bother us, but that should be grounds for us to pray for the leadership rather than to criticise them. Sadly, critical people seldom pray.

Paul's requests for prayer to his prayer-partners provide helpful guidance in praying for those serving and proclaiming the Lord Jesus:

- Deliverance from malicious unbelievers.
- Acceptance with God's people.
- Health of mind and body.
- The ability to speak the right words boldly at the moment of opportunity.

If we pray biblical petitions like these we may be sure of interceding according to the will of God, and equally sure that God will answer.

Characteristics of intelligent intercessory prayer

An important aid to intelligent intercession is given in Hebrews 13:3: 'Remember those in prison *as if you were their fellow-prisoners*, and those who are ill-treated *as if you yourselves were suffering'* (my emphasis). It helps us to pray intelligently if we picture in our mind each person for whom we pray and try to put ourselves into their situation as far as we know it.

Paul's instructions to Timothy regarding intercession also contain a word we may easily overlook: 'I urge, then, first of all, that requests, prayers, intercession and *thanksgiving* be made for everyone' (my italics).

There are occasions when we may find ourselves predisposed to criticism rather than commendation, finding it easier to pick holes than to be constructive. Intercession can then, if we are not careful, become a kind of critical lecture to God about our fellow believers. That is a frightening possibility. The effort to thank God for every good thing we see in those for whom we pray provides a healthy corrective against this peril. It will cause us to rejoice before God because of His grace and power seen in the lives of so many. Interceding correctly for others means praying positively for them. Negative praying is not really intercession at all.

The Holy Spirit's special help in prompting our intercession

A formidable list of restrictions that might hinder us from praying properly could easily be compiled, For example, we could mention our ignorance of the future, the lack of understanding at times we have of our own needs, and the waywardness of our hearts that would prompt us to pray frequently with false motives.

At the very point of our weaknesses, however, the Holy Spirit can help us. The varying nature of our circumstances presents no problem to Him; nothing ever takes Him by surprise. His help is always specific to our situation. Nowhere is this more wonderful than when we give ourselves to prayer.

The Holy Spirit prompts or urges us to pray for the right things. Here His help is right on target, for our main difficulty is that at times we do not even know how to pray. There are times when the Holy Spirit places particular burdens upon us for individuals. He also helps us to express those feelings in the right manner: He 'intercedes for [us] in accordance with God's will' (Rom. 8:27). Having given us right views of God and of His promises, He prompts prayers and requests for those benefits it is God's purpose to give. Without our realising it, He puts requests and words into our mouths, not as His, but as our own.

Then there are those times when prayer is difficult. When we do not feel like praying is the very time we need to pray most, and when the Holy Spirit is most conspicuously our helper.

The words of one of William Cowper's hymns are worth reading aloud and praying for them to be our experience:

> *Prayer makes the darkest cloud withdraw,*
> *Prayer climbs the ladder Jacob saw;*
> *Gives exercise to faith and love,*
> *Brings every blessing from above.*
>
> *Restraining prayer, we cease to fight;*
> *Prayer makes the Christians armour bright;*
> *And Satan trembles when he sees*
> *The weakest saint upon his knees.*[4]

A PRAYER TO BE AN ACTIVE INTERCESSOR

Heavenly Father, thank You for all those people who have prayed for me over many years, and those who do so now. Help me to be faithful in intercession for others and to be sensitive to the promptings of Your Spirit. Enable me to wrestle in prayer that all whom I know, whether at home or abroad, may stand firm in all Your will for them. I worship You with amazement and thanksgiving that You can answer immeasurably more than all I ask or imagine. I thank You in my Saviour's Name. Amen.

J IS FOR JOY

Sadly, joy is not commonly associated with old age. We can easily become grumpy old men and women. But for those who know what it is to be reconciled to God through our Lord Jesus Christ's atoning work, and to be adopted into God's family, our lives should be marked by a unique joy.

Joy tends to arise from an agreeable set of circumstances, such as a hospital visit proving that what was thought to be wrong is not the case. It may be the joy of family and its younger members wanting to visit us. But these things are not everyday experiences and, at best, passing joys.

The joy we can know as Christians is a joy springing up within us, irrespective of our circumstances or difficulties. Paul and Silas are good examples. In Philippi they were imprisoned. Yet, although beaten and bleeding, with their feet in prison stocks, at midnight they were found praying and singing psalms (Acts 16:25). Joy is a gift of

God through our Lord Jesus Christ, and one of the principal consequences of the salvation He gives.

The essence of Christian joy

Such Christian joy contains the following hallmarks:

- Its distinctive feature is that it is joy in God Himself through our Lord Jesus. He has been the anticipated joy of the ages – Abraham and others rejoiced at the thought of seeing His day (John 8:56; cf. 1 Pet. 1:10–12).
- God the Holy Spirit delights to convey this joy in the Lord Jesus to a believer's soul, a glorious joy that is a foretaste of heaven (1 Pet. 4:13; Jude 24).
- It is inexpressible since it is incapable of adequate explanation in words (1 Pet. 1:8).
- It is an everlasting joy to be experienced in all its perfection in heaven (Is. 35:10; 51:11).

The solid foundations of Christian joy

This Christian joy is also built on these truths:

- It arises from our having been found by the Good Shepherd, our Saviour Jesus Christ, and discovering in Him a treasure beyond price. C.S. Lewis significantly entitled his autobiography *Surprised by Joy*.

- It is the joy of faith in a once crucified Saviour, now risen and ascended. While having not yet seen Him, we believe in Him and are filled with inexpressible joy – a joy that expresses itself in heartfelt song, as in John Newton's hymn:

How sweet the Name of Jesus sounds
In a believer's ear!
It soothes his sorrows, heals his wounds,
And drives away his fear ...

Dear Name, the rock on which I build,
My shield and Hiding Place,
My never failing treasury, filled
With boundless stores of grace![5]

I have made it a habit to read – or better still, to sing – a hymn or song before my daily Bible reading. I have to admit that I now croak like a frog rather than sing as a nightingale! But invariably it does my soul good and my cup overflows with joy!

It is the joy of salvation: forgiveness; reconciliation with God; justification through faith; acceptance with God; the privilege of calling God 'Father'; and knowing fellowship with the Father and with His Son, our Saviour, through the ministry of the Holy Spirit to our soul.

It is also the joy of fellowship with our Christian brothers and sisters because it flows from our fellowship with God.

It is the joy of looking forward to sharing God's glory and participation in our Saviour's ultimate triumph when every knee will bow to Him in heaven and on earth and under the earth, and every tongue confess that He is Lord, to the glory of God the Father (Phil. 2:10–11).

The centrality of our Lord Jesus in our joy

A great truth to grasp about Christian joy is that it is the joy of our Lord Jesus Christ in us. Christian joy at its best is the Lord Jesus sharing His joy with us as He completely shares our life (Rev. 3:20). The Lord Jesus said to His disciples,

As the Father has loved me, so have I loved you. Now remain in my love. If you obey my commands, you will remain in my love, just as I have obeyed my Father's commands and remain in his love. I have told you this so that my joy may be in you and that your joy may be complete (John 15:9–11).

Our Saviour wants us to have the full measure of His joy within us, exactly as He wanted for His first disciples (John 17:13). His joy was obedience to the Father's will, at whatever cost; our joy is to be the joy of daily obedience to God's will as we find it unfolded in His Word.

Our joy will express itself in praise and thanksgiving to God, together with confidence in Him and in the strength He gives. Thus our joy will not only survive difficult circumstances – including those of old age – but almost seem to thrive on them, because of the joyful perspective of faith that God can use every difficulty and obstacle to mature and perfect the development of His Son's character in us.

Our joy is maintained as our faith grows and we fix our eyes upon the Lord Jesus, rejoicing in the prospect of sharing in His glory. It is sustained as we continually rediscover the perfection of God's peace through the exercise of prayer.

Snares that spoil our joy

We have seen all that is wonderful about our joy in the Lord Jesus Christ, but what can ruin this? We need to watch out for the following:

- Failure to make progress in our faith – whereas the older we get the stronger it ought to be.
- Neglecting to aim always at doing what is the right thing – practical righteousness.
- Not taking the trouble to seek peace in human relationships, causing breakdowns in loving each other as our Saviour commanded.
- Unbelief, as we listen to the world rather than to God.
- Neglecting prayer and meditation on God's Word.
- Unconfessed sin that grieves God the Holy Spirit.

A PRAYER TO BE FILLED WITH JOY

Lord Jesus, whenever I lose my joy in You, help me to hear You knocking at the door of my life. Help me to respond so that You fully share my life and are my joy. Amen.

K IS FOR KNOWLEDGE

If we are Christians, our conversion and new birth took place as 'God, who said, "Let light shine out of darkness," made his light shine in our hearts to give us the light of the knowledge of the glory of God in the face of Christ' (2 Cor. 4:6). The Holy Spirit, who works this miracle in our life, delights then to reveal more and more to us about our Lord and Saviour through our reading and hearing of the Scriptures.

Know the Lord Jesus

Every day we should come to the Scriptures wanting to find the Lord Jesus there. What we know of or about Him must not leave our affections behind. Head knowledge alone is not enough; we need heart knowledge of Him too.

Our heart's desire should be that of the apostle Paul: 'I want to know Christ and the power of his resurrection and the fellowship of sharing in his sufferings, becoming like him in his death' (Phil. 3:10). Each word of this desire deserves to be pondered.

The privilege of knowing our Lord Jesus humbles us more and more. We then cherish His Name as we daily think of all that He is and all He is for us, and then honour Him by both our speech and way of life.

There are many other ways in which this word 'know' is important, but the three that follow are immediately relevant to our old age.

Know how fleeting life is

David wrote, 'Show me, O LORD, my life's end and the number of my days; let me know how fleeting is my life' (Ps. 39:4). This knowledge should lead us to live carefully, not leaving undone the most important things. Life is running out on us. Perhaps relationships have broken down between us and people who once were close friends or members of our wider family. Do not count on future time to put things right; do it now! Perhaps there is someone close to us with whom we have never shared the good news of our Saviour. Do not reckon on having plenty of time to do so.

Know what the Lord requires of you

'And what does the LORD require of you? To act justly and to love mercy and to walk humbly with your God' (Mic. 6:8). Let's look at each of those aspects in turn.

1. We are to act justly

This means to do what is morally right in all our relationships. As parents, grandparents, great-grandparents, aunts and uncles we are to love, educate and care for all the members of our family, putting their interests before our own. A snare of old age is thinking that our family owes us care and concern. While that may be so, it does family relationships little good if we become demanding. It is better to expect nothing and then to be surprised and grateful when we receive much from them.

As citizens, we are to be exemplary citizens, whatever the colour, politics or race of our fellow citizens. As members of God's family, we are to care for one another, but also for all whose needs we are able to relieve. We are to act justly – in other words, these imperatives are not to be theory but practice.

2. We are to love mercy

The Good Samaritan in our Lord Jesus' parable is an example of this (Luke 10:25–37). There we learn mercy is *seeing* the need of someone even if others ignore it (vv. 31–33). It is *taking pity* upon a person when we see his or her need (v. 33). It is being *practical* in our help (v. 34). It is providing whatever help we can (vv. 34–35).

Mercy inspires *a gentle spirit*, even if by nature we are not gentle. See the Samaritan 'pouring on oil and wine' (v. 34) – mercy sets no limits to its desire to help. Notice also how we are to love mercy, to delight in it.

3. We are to walk with God

(We consider this later under the letter W.) To walk humbly with God is to live always with an awareness of what He did for us by His Son's atoning death. It is to acknowledge daily our sins and our dependence upon His forgiveness. Aim to keep short accounts with God. Walking humbly with God we do what is right not to gain the applause or approval of people around us but for His alone.

Know what to do when you are afraid

All stages of life hold fears but they become more acute in old age when we are aware that our physical and mental powers are diminishing, and that there is little that we can do about it.

We may fear increasing weakness, leading to our having to abandon our home to be in a care home. We may fear pain and the sudden discovery of a life-threatening disease like cancer. We may fear becoming a burden upon those whom we love. We may fear disgracing ourselves by some stupidity due to old age.

What then should we do? Listen to David's answer: 'When I am afraid, I will trust in you.' And he adds the grounds of that confidence: 'whose word I praise' (Ps. 56:3–4). David had never found God's promises to fail.

Why is knowledge so important in old age?

If we have not attained to some level of knowledge and wisdom in old age, it is unlikely that we ever shall!

Although as we get older our brains slow down, our knowledge and experience more than make up for it when it comes to the ability to give good advice (Job 12:12).

We can be a special channel through which God's wisdom may be shared with those who are younger because of what God has graciously taught us from His Word over the years.

A PRAYER FOR KNOWING THE LORD JESUS BETTER

Thank You, Father, for helping me to understand that I only discover my real reason for existence as I learn to praise You through Jesus Christ, Your Son and my Saviour. I bow in wonder before Your amazing wisdom revealed in the plan of salvation, and I thank You that Your salvation has become real in my life. Please keep on enlightening the eyes of my heart so that knowing You better I may praise You better. Help me to enjoy praising You so much that I may honestly anticipate the joys of heaven. I ask this for the praise of Your Name and in the Name of the Lord Jesus Christ. Amen.

L IS FOR LOVE

When there is a power cut, the refrigerator and the TV stop working, and the lights and heating go off. They all require the dynamic power of electricity. Love is the dynamic power of Christian character and life. When love is in place, everything else slots into position.

Our starting place is God's character

The Bible affirms that 'God is love' (1 John 4:8,16). This does not mean that God is only love, but it points to love as one of His major characteristics, along with the important attribute or quality of holiness. The apostle John declares, therefore, that God is both love and light (1 John 1:5; 4:16).

The New Testament always takes us to the cross of our Lord Jesus Christ as the greatest demonstration and proof of God's love. He sent His one and only Son into the world with the specific purpose of becoming the atoning sacrifice for our sins. The death of Christ is the Bible's hub. To consider it, and to recognise our dependence upon the saving work of our Lord Jesus, is like pressing the automatic focus button on a camera. With the cross as the focal point, all else finds its proper focus.

As we fix our eyes upon our Saviour's death for us, we grow in our appreciation of God's love. To properly esteem this love, we must constantly ponder it. God always loves us with the intensity of love seen at Calvary.

At the same time we should grasp our Lord Jesus' love for us. At the heart of Christian experience is this profound truth: 'The life I live in the body, I live by faith in the Son of God, who loved me and gave himself for me' (Gal. 2:20).

Two passages in the gospels illustrate the practical and glorious nature of our Saviour's love. The first is the account of the illness and death of Lazarus (John 11). The record of Jesus' love for Lazarus and his two sisters assures us of His love for us likewise as individuals.

The second is how, on the night Jesus was forsaken by the disciples, 'Having loved his own who were in the world, he now showed them the full extent of his love' (John 13:1) in spite of all their failures.

Our Saviour's love for us is the required pattern and model of the love we are in turn to show to others since Jesus said, 'A new command I give you: Love one another. As I have loved you, so you must love one another' (John 13:34).

Satisfaction and security in God's love

The foremost characteristic of godly men and women throughout the centuries has been their appreciation of God's love and its reflection in their lives – the two are inseparable.

The Holy Spirit's unique prerogative is to reveal to our souls the love God has for us. Usually He does this by means of His own Word, as we read it or hear it taught and preached. We find ourselves saying, whatever our circumstances, 'we know and rely on the love God has for us' (1 John 4:16).

Significantly, the Lord Jesus spoke to early Christians of their 'first love' for Him (Rev. 2:4). The initial experience of the forgiveness of our sins produces a great burst of love for God that hopefully grows as we grasp more and more of that love's infinite dimensions.

The more we love God, the more we know Him to be our best possession, the chief happiness and joy of our soul (Ps. 16:2). No peace or rest compares with resting in God's love.

Love in action

There is, though, a vital consequence of appreciating this love. The most important way to show to the world that we are God's children and disciples of His Son is to display His love for others through our conduct. It is not enough to say to people, 'God loves you.' Our behaviour must prove it. Love is the one continuing debt we owe to one another (Rom. 13:8).

Love's priority is all the greater when we recognise that the love we express to others is the love we show to the Lord Jesus. There will be many delightful surprises on the Day of Judgment when He says to some, 'whatever you did for one of the least of these brothers of mine, you did for me' (Matt. 25:40).

Love sees all other Christians as brothers and sisters, and all who are not Christians as neighbours. This is not without effort – effort that God's Spirit inspires. This love is not so much a question of our feelings, but a matter of will and action – a principle by which we live. It does not ask, 'Do I like or love this person?' but rather, 'How may I act in love towards him or her?'

Love is the permanent priority of the Christian life, to inform and dictate every action. It remains the principal test of our Christian profession. I need to identify honestly the people I find it most difficult to love. Then I need to commit myself to praying for them daily, and to seek their well-being by specific acts of love. Every time I meet around the Lord's Table I should re-examine my love – my love for my Saviour Jesus Christ and for others.

Why is love so important in old age?

Self-examination of my character must begin here since love is the most prominent and powerful aspect of the fruit of the Spirit. Why not read again 1 Corinthians 13?

While physical ability diminishes, love can be exercised all our lifetime by prayer for others, thoughtfulness, caring and patience.

Even as well-established fruit trees often provide the best fruit, so older Christians should produce the best examples of God's love in a Christlike life.

A PRAYER FOR LAVISH LOVE

I bow in worship, Father, at the truth that You so loved the world that You gave Your only Son to be our Saviour. I cannot understand why You should love someone so sinful as I am, and yet I know it is true. Please help me to love as You have loved me, to give to others as You have given to me, and may Your love seen in me draw others to You. For Jesus Christ's sake. Amen.

M IS FOR MEDITATE

Meditation has a unique place in godliness. Often mentioned in the Book of Psalms, the first mention in the New Testament is Mary's reaction when truths about her Son were revealed at His birth: 'Mary treasured up all these things and *pondered* them in her heart' (Luke 2:19, my italics).

What is meditation?

We are probably familiar with the term 'transcendental meditation'. This finds its origin in Eastern religions based upon the idea that the source of salvation is found within us, and that we need to find inner forms of consciousness in order to discover a secret inner divinity. This is *not* what the Bible means.

Writing of the dangers of false teaching, Paul reminds us that 'Satan himself masquerades as an angel of light' (2 Cor. 11:14). God is not an impersonal being whom we may access in some way through ways of sitting, breathing and emptying ourselves of thought. Rather it is seeing God's face in Jesus Christ, discovering Him to be the Heavenly Father who made us and who has given us the glorious possibility and privilege of knowing Him as such, and enjoying Him for ever.

An example of meditation

In the early 1960s Robert Kennedy, President Kennedy's brother, visited Brazil. While there he was introduced by a Wycliffe Bible translator to an Amazonian Indian who had recently come to know the Lord Jesus as his Saviour. 'Ask him what he enjoys most,' Kennedy asked, expecting him to say hunting with bows and arrows or canoeing. He was more than a little surprised by the Indian's response: 'Being occupied with God.' 'Ask him again,' the Senator requested, thinking that his question had been misunderstood. The Indian gave the same answer!

Meditation is, at its heart, being occupied with God as we deliberately ponder truth about Him and His will that the Scriptures reveal. It does not happen by accident; it is something we choose and determine to do as we make God's Word our delight.

Think of a bee seeking honey. Thomas Brooks wrote, 'It is not the bee's touching of the flower that gathers honey, but her abiding for a time upon the flower that draws out the sweet. It is not he that reads most, but he that meditates the most, that will prove the choicest, sweetest, wisest and strongest Christian.'[6]

Why should we meditate?

There are several reasons why we greatly profit from meditation.

Meditation on God's Word increases our understanding of it and its application to life, bringing growing blessing to our soul

John Bunyan, a writer of good books, therefore warned against giving books precedence over meditating upon God's Word. He wrote,

> Although you may have no commentaries at hand, continue to read the Word and pray; for a little from God is better than a great deal received from man. Too many are content to listen to what comes from men's mouths, without searching and kneeling before God to know the real truth. That which we

receive directly from the Lord through the study of His Word is from the 'minting house' itself. Even old truths are new if they come to us with the smell of heaven upon them.

Meditation protects our minds against unhelpful thoughts

We might have imagined that the latter would not be so much of a problem when we get older. But Satan knows how to bring back the remembrance of our past failures and sins. The more we fill our minds with the good things God has taught us, the greater will be our resistance and victory.

Meditation should focus on the person of our Lord Jesus Christ

Meditation upon His Person and work is a protection against spiritual decay as fluoride is to tooth decay. But it is more than protection; it is a tonic to our soul's well-being and a joy and comfort in times of stress and difficulty.

When should we meditate?

We've established that meditating is vital, but how often should we do so?

Meditate daily

The first psalm, that in many ways is the key to our understanding of all the psalms, reminds us that the godly find their delight in the law of the Lord and meditate on it day and night (v. 2).

Vary the amount according to the time of day

In planning the times we give to meditation it is important to consider which part of the day we will be most attentive to the Bible's teaching. My thinking ability is at its best in the morning after I have breakfasted. Late in the evening, approaching bedtime, my concentration diminishes. So recently my pattern is to allow plenty of time in the morning for my Bible reading and prayer. I end each day with the day's reading in Charles Spurgeon's *Cheque Book of the Bank of Faith,* and then commit my family, friends and myself to God for the night.

Once we have found a helpful pattern, we should stick to it so that its priority is not diminished. However, it does no harm to change the way we do things from time to time if we feel our current practice has become a matter of routine rather than a delight.

How should we meditate?

Inevitably the next question is how exactly we should meditate upon God's Word:

- It needs to be deliberate.
- It is best done unhurriedly, with no eye on the clock.
- It should focus on that passage of the Scripture we have arrived at in our daily systematic reading of the Bible.
- It is helpful to write down Scripture verses that have stood out and directed us to something we need to keep always in mind.
- Perhaps precede your Bible reading by reading – or sometimes singing – a hymn or a psalm.
- Meditation is enhanced by writing down helpful truths that come to us as we listen to the teaching and preaching of God's Word. I always carry in my pocket a little notebook in which I can write down something said, sung or read that holds a truth I want to remember and meditate upon.

A PRAYER FOR A MORE MEDITATIVE HEART

Lord, may the words of my mouth and the meditation of my heart be pleasing in Your sight, as I rejoice in You. I ask this in the Name of my Saviour. Amen.

N IS FOR
NON-JUDGMENTAL

A peril of old age is jumping to wrong conclusions and passing judgment as we recall earlier days and say, 'Things are not like what they used to be.' We can become negative and suspicious of anything that takes us out of our comfort zone. We then become like a piece of grit that irritates and hinders the smooth running of things rather than being lubricating oil promoting harmony.

As we grow older, we inevitably – at some point – become dependent upon the help of others. But we may misjudge them because we feel that they do not give us sufficient time. Perhaps nurses or carers turn up late or rush their tasks, allowing little time for meaningful conversation – something we so much miss. We then complain to our friends of the poor standard of treatment we have received.

And then what of our opinions about church? Particular issues raise their heads, not least music and sometimes the way church life has changed: hymn books replaced by words on a screen, the organ discarded, and pews replaced by seats. How easy it is to become grumpy old men and women!

Hannah was misjudged by Eli, when he mistook her praying for drunkenness. I wonder if you have ever been in the position in which I admit I have been. Having seen a young couple getting married, you anticipate hearing in due course that they have children. Years pass, the situation does not change and your sinful heart suggests, 'They do not want children,' or, 'Their careers and independence rule out the possibility of the responsibility of parenthood.' And then suddenly one of two things happens! They announce with indescribable joy, 'We are going to have a baby, something we have always wanted!' Or, on the other hand, they appear with a young child, without any pregnancy – they have gone through the long and difficult process of adoption. Their joy is equal to that of any other couple! And, sadly, we had been judgmental, thinking the worst rather than the best.

Show mercy

When we engage in negative and condemnatory thought or conversation, mercy flies out of the window. Ringing in my ears are God's Word to His people through the prophet Micah: 'And what does the LORD require of you? To act justly and to love mercy and to walk humbly with your God' (Mic. 6:8). In springing to criticise and judge, we act unjustly, forget mercy and walk proudly like the devil.

The early disciples were not immune from judgmentalism: 'Teacher ... we saw a man driving out demons in your name and we told him to stop, because he was not one of us' (Mark 9:38). Notice that little word 'us'. We may foolishly judge other Christians by the songs that they sing, the translation of the Bible they use, or the type of church government they practise, if it is different from our own practices.

The Lord Jesus took trouble in the Sermon on the Mount to correct the disciples' perceptions – and ours. He said,

Do not judge, or you too will be judged. For in the same way as you judge others, you will be judged, and with the measure you use, it will be measured to you.

Why do you look at the speck of sawdust in your brother's eye and pay no attention to the plank in your own eye? How can you say to your brother, 'Let me take the speck out of your eye,' when all the time there is a plank in your own eye? You hypocrite, first take the plank out of your own eye, and then you will see clearly to remove the speck from your brother's eye (Matt. 7:1–5).

Remember God's grace to us

Being judgmental is the fruit of a heart that is out of tune with God. Think of the elder brother in the parable of the prodigal son who said to his father, 'Look! All these years I've been slaving for you and never disobeyed your orders. Yet you never gave me even a young goat so I could celebrate with my friends. But when this son of yours who has squandered your property with prostitutes comes home, you kill the fattened calf for him!' (Luke 15:29–30). The more we stand in judgment of others the less we show the grace of God in our own life.

Is there ever a place for exercising judgment?

There are, though, times when judgment is an appropriate response:

If it concerns serious misbehaviour of fellow believers, judgment and discipline are to be exercised by those called to be our spiritual leaders. The judgment of sin within the church requires a corporate rather than a personal judgment.

If the conduct that worries us is of someone close to us, it may be that it is right, after prayer, to say to them that we feel concerned for them. In the context of human relationships, 'Wounds from a friend can be trusted' (Prov. 27:6).

However, if the behaviour that concerns us is of those who are not Christians, then we must remember that it is not our business to judge those outside the church. Paul asks, 'What business is it of mine to judge those outside the church? Are you not to judge those inside? God will judge those outside' (1 Cor. 5:12–13).

It is also easy to fall into the snare of thinking that everyone who has a different understanding from ours is totally defective in understanding. We must love all who love the Lord Jesus in sincerity. This is not to suggest that doctrine does not matter – in fact, the opposite. But we do not diminish our hold of the faith by being gracious to those whose views and understanding may be different from ours.

Why is judgmentalism to be guarded against in old age?

- It puts up barriers and ruins relationships, particularly between different age groups.
- It is better, by God's grace, to be an instrument of His peace than a member of Satan's fifth column.
- To grow old graciously is to choose to sit upon the seat of love instead of the seat of judgment.

A PRAYER AGAINST JUDGMENTALISM

Father, as I examine my life in the light of Your Word, I recognise that sometimes I have been all too quick to judge others and slow to judge my own actions. I ask for Your forgiveness. Help me to remember the example of my Saviour, Your dear Son, and to imitate His mindset in all those daily situations where I may be tempted to rush into proud and foolish criticism and judgment. I ask this in Jesus' Name. Amen.

O IS FOR OBEDIENCE

The idea of obedience to God is not immediately pleasant to fallen men and women, the descendants of Adam and Eve. To obey God seems to be restrictive and forbidding, almost insanity, some might say. It appears contrary to our human freedom and something that may diminish our enjoyment of life. In fact, the opposite is the case!

It is the enemy of souls, who misled our first parents in the Garden of Eden, who perpetuates this lie. How we view obedience to God indicates how real our relationship and fellowship with Him is. A key evidence of spiritual new birth is delighting to do what God wants.

When the apostle Peter begins his first letter, writing to both Jewish and Gentile believers scattered throughout the ancient world, the four things they had in common through their identical relationship to the Lord Jesus were that they had been 'chosen according to the foreknowledge of God the Father, through the sanctifying work of the Spirit, *for obedience to Jesus Christ* and sprinkling by his blood' (1 Pet. 1:2, my italics). Obedience to the Lord Jesus was, and is, the evidence of God at work in a human life.

Our initial obedience is to *the gospel* (Rom. 1:16) and to *the faith* (Acts 6:7), having discovered that the Lord Jesus is 'the source of eternal salvation for all who obey him' (Heb. 5:9). Being a Christian is honestly responding to the teaching from God's Word that first brought us into a right relationship to God (Rom. 6:17; Acts 2:42).

An important distinction

Christian obedience is uniquely different from all other forms of obedience. It is not so much an obedience to *gain* God's favour but an obedience *because* of His favour to us. God does not accept us primarily because we are obedient, much as our new-found obedience pleases Him. He accepts us – and saves us – *by the obedience of our Lord Jesus Christ*, an obedience that brought Him into the world, that He exhibited in every part of His earthly life and that took Him to the cross to die for our disobedience to God.

Obedience is the essence of our daily relationship to God as His spiritual children. As we look back upon our human childhood, from the very beginning we were taught to be obedient to our parents. Yet while they may have erred in their demands and requirements of us, our Heavenly Father does not. Part of the wonderful experience of new birth is God sending the Spirit of His Son into our hearts – His Son who said, 'The one who sent me is with me; he has not left me alone, for I always do what pleases him' (John 8:29). The Holy Spirit not only helps us to cry, '*Abba*, Father', but also helps us to delight to do what pleases our Father. For God wants us to meet with Him every time we read His Word and our proper response is to declare, 'Speak, Lord, and I will obey.'

A reasonable response to grace

Our obedience to God as Christian believers is our spontaneous and reasonable response to His grace to us in His Son. This explains why Paul begins his powerful chapter twelve of his letter to the Romans with the words, 'Therefore, I urge you, brothers, *in view of God's mercy*, to offer your bodies as living sacrifices, holy and pleasing to God – this is your spiritual act of worship' (12:1, my italics). While it is true that God commands us to do many things, the reason we obey Him is because we now love Him and are daily grateful for all that He has done for us in our Saviour. When we are slow in obedience, it is always because we have taken our eyes away from the Lord Jesus and His cross.

The primary mark of the Lord Jesus' sheep is that they listen to His voice and follow Him (John 10:16, 27). The obedience we give to Him is the obedience of faith, and faith and obedience are virtually synonymous (Heb. 11:8).

An unconscious witness

It is by our joyful obedience that we show people who have no knowledge of God how good it is to serve such a wonderfully kind and wise Master. Satan deceives the world by suggesting that obedience to God can never bring happiness; our lives should demonstrate that the opposite is the truth. As old people, we should be able to give unique testimony to the blessing of obedience, a truth this old hymn reflects:

When we walk with the Lord
In the light of His Word
What a glory He sheds on our way!
While we do His good will,
He abides with us still,
And with all who will trust and obey.

Trust and obey, for there's no other way
To be happy in Jesus, but to trust and obey.

(John H. Sammis)[7]

At every stage of life obedience produces a different way of life and becomes a telling testimony, even as it did in the experience of the Israelites. Moses said to them,

See, I have taught you decrees and laws as the Lord *my God commanded me, so that you may follow them in the land you are entering to take possession of it. Observe them carefully, for this will show your wisdom and understanding to the nations, who will hear about all these decrees and say, 'Surely this great nation is a wise and understanding people'* *(Deut. 4:5–6).*

Obedience's unique benefits

Not only is obedience an appropriate response to the cross and an important testimony, but the Bible also tells us that it is the means of us enjoying blessings:

- It brings the promise of an intimate relationship to our Lord Jesus Christ: 'Whoever does God's will is my brother and sister and mother' (Mark 3:35).
- It provides our life with a unique stability when the storms of life come because it is built upon a solid rock (Matt. 7:24–27).
- It brings the benefits of God's peace to our life like a refreshing river (Is. 48:18).
- It is the road along which we travel to heaven.
- God never calls us to do anything without providing the strength and power we need to obey.

Practical obedience

If we are to delight in doing as God pleases, there are important practical steps that we must take:

- Never listen to teaching and preaching without praying, 'Speak, Lord, for your servant listens.'

- Read the Bible always with a prayer for understanding, and of how that understanding should be shown in obedience.
- Ask God for a sensitive conscience that is quick to obey.

A PRAYER FOR OBEDIENCE

Lord, as I look back over my life, I know that Your will has always been right for me, and that my mistakes are so often the consequence of my disobedience. I want to say 'yes' to Your will before ever I know what it is. Help me so to store up Your Word daily in my heart that I may be like my Saviour, who found His joy in doing Your will. In His Name I ask it. Amen.

P IS FOR PEACEABLE

Old age is all too often associated with anger and grumpiness, and on both sides of the Atlantic television programmes focus upon the crankiness of old men and women. Sadly, there is more than a grain of truth in the caricatures because physical difficulties we increasingly experience may all too easily bring out the worst in us and make us people with whom it is difficult to live harmoniously.

Yet, anger, irritability and touchiness tend to do us more harm than those who are on the receiving end of our displeasure. While anger in all of its forms is harmful to others, it has physical effects upon those who display it, perhaps in sleeplessness and a loss of inner peace. Acts 7:54 describes how those who were angry with Stephen's testimony to Jesus began grinding their teeth at him in their rage. Their hostility did them harm. Whereas Stephen saw heaven open and the Lord Jesus ready to receive him (v. 55), his opponents disclosed the sinfulness of their own hearts.

The challenge is that in old age we tend to grow more like ourselves. In other words, if we were grumpy in our youth or middle age, the likelihood is that we become more so the older we get. Some of the features of our character may be inherited from our parents or influenced by unhelpful friendships.

An expected change

However, the wonderful experience of new birth brings both the desire and God-given ability to change as we are called to be like the Lord Jesus, through the help of the Spirit of God living within us. We are encouraged to remember and to be 'confident … that he who began a good work in [us] will carry it on to completion until the day of Christ Jesus' (Phil. 1:6).

If we enter a potter's workshop, we will probably see a variety of the potter's workmanship all at different stages of completion. That is true of our life too. As the prophet Isaiah writes, 'O LORD, you are our Father. We are the clay, you are the potter; we are all the work of your hand' (Is. 64:8). Rather than growing more like ourselves as we grow older, we should be growing more like the Lord Jesus to our dying day.

A vital and indispensable practice is fixing our eyes upon the Lord Jesus and His example (Phil. 2:1–8) and by praying specifically about every challenge to our character and behaviour. Then, and only then, will the peace of God, which surpasses all understanding, guard our hearts and minds in Christ Jesus (Phil. 4:7).

A required effort

The Book of Proverbs counsels us, 'Do not make friends with a hot-tempered man, do not associate with one easily angered, or you may learn his ways and get yourself ensnared' (22:24–25). Peaceableness is to be aimed at in all the relationships of life and is an essential counterpart or complement of practical holiness: 'Make every effort to live in peace with all men and to be holy', the writer to the Hebrews urges upon his readers (Heb. 12:14). Peter does the same: 'Whoever would love life and see good days must keep his tongue from evil and his lips from deceitful speech. He must turn from evil and do good; he must seek peace and pursue it' (1 Pet. 3:10–11).

With gentle answers we may turn away people's anger (Prov. 15:1). We are to remember that 'there is a future for the man of peace' (Ps. 37:37).

Peaceableness is not only 'of great worth in God's sight' but it has its own unfading beauty and attractiveness (1 Pet. 3:3–4).

Honest questions requiring honest answers

If we are to be peaceable, we need to sincerely and humbly ponder these questions:

- How do people think of us? Are we sometimes like a hot, spitting frying pan or like a warm, comforting and reassuring fire?
- When there is an argument do we, by our presence, either add fuel to the flame or do we promote reasonable discussion with a calming presence?
- If your family or local church family were suddenly beset by disunity or disagreement, would its members look to you for mediation – or at least to be a moderating influence?

Why is peaceableness so important in old age?

- It is good for us health-wise: 'A heart at peace gives life to the body' (Prov. 14:30).

- If we have genuinely grown spiritually, we will be examples of peaceableness.
- It is a benefit we can contribute to the body of Christ to the end of our earthly life, without holding any office or visible responsibility.
- It is a foremost mark of God's wisdom in us (Jas. 3:17–18).
- As older people, we may sometimes sense or observe tensions between members of our family. We are frequently in a position to say or do something positive and constructive about it, as others are not.
- When we want to be peaceable in any situation of conflict, we may know that the God of peace will be with us – a wonderful blessing!
- Irrespective of age, 'Peacemakers who sow in peace raise a harvest of righteousness' (Jas. 3:18).
- Those who plan and promote peace have joy (Prov. 12:20).

A PRAYER FOR A PEACEABLE CHARACTER

I rejoice, LORD, that You are the God of peace, otherwise I would not have the confidence to come before You. I freely and gladly acknowledge that I do so with confidence because of Your Son's atoning sacrifice for sinners like me. Make me an instrument of Your peace in my home, among my friends, my neighbours and Your people.

If there are relationships I need to repair or apologies to make, grant me now the will and grace to be obedient. I want to pray the words of the old chorus:

Let the beauty of Jesus be seen in me,
All His wonderful passion and purity;
O my Saviour divine, all my being refine,
Till the beauty of Jesus be seen in me.[8]

(Albert Orsborn)

Amen.

Q IS FOR QUICKNESS

When it comes to physical activity, quickness is something that it is perilous in old age to make a priority. I dare not run for a bus any longer! I must not hurry on to an escalator in a store. Both hurrying and speed lead to accidents and danger. However, there are areas of life where it is appropriate to be quick.

Quick to obey

David writes, 'I will hasten and not delay to obey your commands' (Ps. 119:60). Immediately before these words he has said to the Lord, 'You are my portion, O Lord; I have promised to obey Your words. I have sought your face with all my heart; be gracious to me according to Your promise. I have considered my ways and have turned my steps to Your statutes' (Ps. 119:57–59). Let's notice what these words say about David's relationship to God:

- The Lord was his portion – all that he needed.
- He saw that obedience to God's Word is so important that it requires commitment to reading and hearing it.
- To read God's Word, properly understood, is to seek His face – just as when we talk to people, we instinctively turn our face towards them if we want to listen to what they say.
- To engage in this spiritual activity will always reveal failings and faults that prompt and demand daily repentance.
- The right response, therefore, is to hasten and not delay in obedience. This is not a miserable thing to do; rather it enables us to live in the enjoyment of God, so much so that we know Him to be our portion – that is to say, the One in whom we find our greatest joy and satisfaction and in whose service is our delight.

Quick to avoid strife

Solomon rightly stated, 'It is to a man's honour to avoid strife, but every fool is quick to quarrel' (Prov. 20:3). Relationships can be ruined in a second by an outburst of anger. Sometimes we may stupidly allow ourselves to be provoked to anger, which overflows into unwise words and actions. We then reach the point where we do not listen to others as we ought (Jas. 1:19).

How good are we at listening to God's voice as we read the Scriptures or hear them preached? And how attentively are we listening to what our brothers and sisters in God's family say to us?

Quick to examine oneself

Self-examination is more important than our examining other people's conduct. The Lord Jesus asks, 'Why do you look at the speck of sawdust in your brother's eye and pay no attention to the plank in your own eye?' (Matt. 7:3).

This priority of quickness in self-examination is to be exercised whenever we come to the Lord's Table and take bread and wine in remembrance of our Saviour's death in our place for the forgiveness of our sins. The Lord's Supper should be a time for self-examination (1 Cor. 11:28).

Quick to pray

Prayer is another area of our life in which to be quick. When we read, hear or watch the daily news, we will be presented with an agenda for prayer long before our friends many miles away may be able to report it to us.

Prayer should always be our first response to any need of which we become aware. If we are with other Christians, we should be quick to suggest prayer. It is a helpful rule never to discuss any subject of concern with another Christian without at the same time suggesting praying about it together.

Quick to speak of the Lord Jesus

I wonder if your experience is similar to mine when I say that with our Christian brothers and sisters we may readily talk about church matters, or people or any number of things, but we do not talk much about our Lord Jesus. When did we last share with another Christian a truth about Him that we had just discovered or rediscovered?

We need to be quick to seize opportunities of bearing testimony to our experience of knowing the Lord Jesus: 'Always be prepared to give an answer to everyone who asks you to give the reason for the hope that you have' (1 Pet. 3:15). That demands praying daily for alertness to opportunities and not letting them take us by surprise. The enemy of souls is subtle in his strategy of making us take our eyes off the Lord Jesus, for he knows who the source of our strength is (Phil. 4:13).

Quick to apologise

Everyone is in need of apologising frequently: 'We all stumble in many ways. If anyone is never at fault in what he says, he is a perfect man, able to keep his whole body in check' (Jas. 3:2). Paul therefore says, '"In your anger do not sin": Do not let the sun go down while you are still angry, and do not give the devil a foothold' (Eph. 4:26–27). Many broken relationships would have been avoided if this guidance and advice had been acted upon.

Quick to give God the praise

People may sometimes be lavish in their praise of us for some reason or another. We would be wise to direct all praise to God. The more we know God, the more we know ourselves and how far short we fall of what we ought to be. Paul plainly lived and walked with God, but he knew himself to be 'the worst' of sinners (1 Tim. 1:15) and that it was by the grace of God he was what he became (1 Cor. 15:10).

Perhaps you can add to the areas in your life where

you need to act more quickly? If so, name them and ask for God's daily help with regard to them.

Why is quickness in so many areas of life important in old age?

- By practising it we bear a good testimony to the Lord Jesus.
- By being quick to do the right thing we do not have a backlog of tasks undone.
- At any stage in life we do not have time on our side, but particularly so in our later years.

A PRAYER FOR QUICKNESS IN OUR CHRISTIAN LIFE

Lord, I am aware of physical activities I have to avoid doing quickly now that I am old. But thank You for daily duties in which I may still be quick. Help me to be quick to praise and acknowledge You when I have the opportunity; at the same time help me to be speedy in saying 'sorry' as well as matching every unkind word I hear with one that brings peace. Help me to be quick in bringing comfort where there is any trace of distress. For Jesus' sake. Amen.

R IS FOR READ

Most of us probably take our ability to read for granted until we find our eyesight diminishing. Yet of equal concern to us should be what we choose to read.

Read the Scriptures

The Bible alone is God's Word: 'All Scripture is God-breathed and is useful for teaching, rebuking, correcting and training in righteousness' (2 Tim. 3:16). Our Christian life began as, through the Scriptures, we were made 'wise for salvation through faith in Christ Jesus' (2 Tim. 3:15).

There are practical steps we can take, though, that will help us in our daily Bible reading.

A fairly large, clear-print Bible is a necessity

Avoid studying the Scriptures with a small-print Bible meant for the pocket rather than for study. We may lose some of the joy of Bible reading if the print is too small.

A notebook is invaluable

If we come to the Scriptures every day wanting God to work in our lives, we will find His Word continually reminding us of truths we have forgotten or giving us fresh understanding. What we write in the notebook is not for anyone else to see, but the mere fact of writing down what we have found helpful will help us to recall something we may need later.

For example, imagine you have arrived at 1 Peter 5 and the relevance of verse 7 stands out: 'Cast all your anxiety on him because he cares for you.' You write it down in your notebook. As the day unfolds, you unexpectedly meet someone that you know. You quickly recognise signs of anxiety. How beneficial it will be if you say, 'Let me share with you what was a blessing to me today as I read 1 Peter 5:7.'

Give adequate time to it

A brief yet regularly devoted period each day reading the Bible is far better and more profitable than numerous resolutions to give long but spasmodic periods to it. The Bible is its own interpreter if we will study it patiently, depending on the Holy Spirit's help.

Remember the Bible is God's Word

The Bible is not just like any other book, or even like a much respected book. It yields its secrets only to those who are prepared to approach it with reverence – with their shoes, as it were, off their feet, and with the desire to obey whatever God says to them through its pages.

Ask daily for the help of the Holy Spirit

You cannot read a sundial without the sun. So it is with us: we cannot do without the light of God's Spirit illuminating our minds as we read.

Read books that will feed your soul

In addition to studying the Scriptures, we learn much from the wisdom of others.

Christian biographies are a rich source of spiritual nourishment

Solomon acutely observed, 'The memory of the righteous will be a blessing' (Prov. 10:7). One person who has been of particular significance for me is Hudson Taylor, the pioneer missionary to China, whose biography was given to me on my twenty-first birthday. I can still repeat word for word the passage that arrested me. A friend wrote to him,

> *How then to have our faith increased? Only by thinking of all that Jesus is, and all He is for us: His life, His death, His work, He Himself as revealed to us in the Word, to be the subject of our constant thoughts. Not a striving to have faith but a looking off to the Loved One entirely, for time and eternity.*[9]

Hebrews 11 underlines the powerful influence the example of godly men and women should have upon our lives. Read as many Christian biographies as you can. I find it helpful, though, to try to balance my reading of Christian biographies with my reading of the life stories of those who do not profess to be Christians. These give insight into how people think and live, while providing much more profitable reading than contemporary fiction.

Devotional writing is beyond price

This is where some of the Puritans shine. I started with *A Body of Divinity* by Thomas Watson. Almost every paragraph contains a spiritual gem. Written much later, Charles Spurgeon's *Cheque Book of the*

Bank of Faith provides brief but incisive comments on a single verse, especially helpful just before going to bed. One of the best books I have found to guide me recently in my daily reading of the Bible is *Through the Year* by John Stott, which is outstanding for its conciseness and clarity.

Read the signs of the times

I find myself horrified at the sad and tragic events in the world, evils that no nation or all nations acting together can control. The Lord Jesus warned His disciples that at some stage the world's problems will be the sign of His coming again and of the end of the age (Matt. 24:3–14).

The key and glorious event we are to anticipate is the return of our Lord Jesus. Beware of speculating about how events will unfold. Find strength and encouragement in the darkest days that God is working out His purposes of calling men and women of all nations to repentance and faith in His Son, our Lord Jesus Christ. God assures us that He has given His Son the name that is above every name, and that one day all shall bow to Him and acknowledge Him as Lord, to the glory of God the Father (Phil. 2:9–11).

Read people's faces

Sadly, as we get older, our own physical well-being may unconsciously dominate our thoughts and make us blind to the needs of others. However, the human face may sometimes be like a page of a book in which human feelings and needs show themselves.

Nehemiah was responsible for serving wine to King Artaxerxes at the time when the Jewish remnant in Judah were in distress and the walls of Jerusalem were broken down. His personal distress was so great that it showed on his face. Never having been sad in the king's presence before, this prompted the king to ask, 'Why does your face look so sad when you are not ill? This can be nothing but sadness of heart' (Neh. 2:2).

May God help us not to be so preoccupied with our own concerns that we neglect reading what the faces of others tell us.

A PRAYER FOR A GREATER 'READING' ABILITY

Lord Jesus, may my face reflect something of my delight in You. Help me to read people's faces, that I may speak a kind and sympathetic word to those whose hearts are sad. Amen.

S IS FOR SERVE

The outstanding title given to our Lord Jesus before His coming into the world was 'the Servant of the Lord'. When He came He took 'the very nature of a servant' (Phil. 2:7). He served His Father perfectly and taught that all who follow Him should emulate His example. Surprising His disciples by washing their feet, He said, 'Now that I, your Lord and Teacher, have washed your feet, you also should wash one another's feet. I have set you an example that you should do as I have done for you' (John 13:14–15).

We may secretly be tempted to think, 'I have made my contribution and now is the time for those younger to do theirs.' But minds transformed by the gospel of our Saviour think of serving rather than being served at every stage of life (Rom. 12:1–2).

Spheres of service

There are a number of areas in which we can serve with such an attitude.

Our neighbourhood

The first is where we live and the people among whom we live. Confident of God's providence, I believe that where we live is not an accident. As we relate to family, friends and neighbours, we may serve them by deliberate thoughtfulness.

Some old people will be housebound because of physical frailty or weather conditions. We may serve them, if we are able, by getting their newspaper, putting out their rubbish or asking if we can do any shopping. Perhaps when we attend a social function, we see someone sitting all alone. We can excuse ourselves from sitting with the people we have chosen to sit with and go and talk to the lonely person. We should not do such simple things to earn thanks, but simply to be of service. As we get to know people better and serve them when we can, opportunities arise for sharing the good news of the Lord Jesus.

Our church

The second sphere of service is the church fellowship to which we belong. Here, again, our circumstances will vary in that some of us may be fit and able to be present regularly, others of us only occasionally and yet others not at all.

Top of the list of our priorities should be the privilege of prayer for the church leadership, the individual members we know, and the work that goes on weekly among the children and young people. If we have missionary members, they should have a special place. When a fellow member visits us, always conclude with prayer for the known needs of the church and its membership. If ever we find some criticism of the church being expressed, learn to say, 'Let's then now pray together about it.'

Our world

The third sphere of service is the world. That perhaps sounds a bit presumptuous! But it is not presumptuous because Paul encourages us to pray 'first of all ... for everyone – for kings and all those in authority, that we may live peaceful and quiet lives in all godliness and holiness. This is good, and pleases God our Saviour, who wants all men to be saved and to come to a knowledge of the truth' (1 Tim. 2:1–4).

Whether we read it in our newspaper, hear it on the radio or watch it on the television, we will gain up-to-date news of what is happening in our own country and the world. Turn what you hear into prayer: it may be praying for flood or hurricane victims, refugees, peace talks where conflict exists or crises at home and abroad. Hidden as we may be, and our prayers unknown to others, God hears them!

We also serve the world by giving to those who represent us in the world by their service and to charities that reach out to those whom we personally cannot physically help. Our giving is a personal matter and not something to be told to others, lest we forget our Saviour's words that our left hand should not know what our right hand does (Matt. 6:3). Once we have established what the proportion of our income it should be, we find that we never miss the money we give.

In our attitude towards others we would do well to emulate John Wesley's advice: 'Do all the good you can. By all means that you can. In all the ways you can. In all the places you can. At all the times you can. To all the people you can. As long as ever you can.'[10]

By sharing the gospel
The final means through which we serve others is by sharing the gospel with them. Paul aimed at being ready to serve *anyone* in the interests of the

gospel, with the longing that he might share with them its blessings (1 Cor. 9:22–23).

In fact, the scope of areas in which we can serve our Lord Jesus is vast. Read Romans 16 and count how many aspects of Christian service are mentioned. I particularly like the way Rufus' mother is described!

Truths to ponder about our service

As we seek to embark upon serving in these ways, we would do well to remember these truths:

- All our service needs to be watered by prayer, just as a gardener sows the seed and then waters it to enable it to grow.
- Our Saviour does not want us to be overburdened in our service; rather He wants to share it with us so that we can honestly say, 'I can do everything through him who gives me strength' (Phil. 4:13).
- The cross is the symbol of service and should be the reason for everything we do. Serving God in a fallen world will not be without difficulties and challenges.
- The best parts of our service are those that only God sees, where we have been willing to

do whatever we can without looking for any approval beyond His.

- We will always feel unworthy servants knowing how great our Master is and how much we owe Him.
- Those closest to their Saviour know best the truth about themselves.

Why not pause just now and ponder the privilege and wealth it is to be a servant of Jesus Christ.

A PRAYER FOR OUR SERVICE

Heavenly Father, right up to my dying day may I discover those good works You have prepared for me to do. For Jesus' sake. Amen.

T IS FOR TALK

To talk is an essential part of daily life. When friends and family get together, the most frequent thing we do is talk! Yet if we live on our own, we may not realise that we are not talking enough.

My doctor once sent me to a hospital consultant about my gruff voice. Surrounded by medical students, she examined my throat and asked, 'Do you live on your own?'

'Yes,' I replied, 'my wife died a few years ago.'

'I think,' she responded, 'the change in your voice is probably because you do not use it as you did when your wife was with you.' That made sense. Some days I may not see anyone with whom to talk. She then asked, 'Do you sing?'

'Yes, I enjoy it, especially hymns.'

'Well, she said, 'sing when you can or read something aloud!'

I now read a hymn every morning, and if I can remember the tune I will sing aloud. My neighbour has not complained, though no choir would have me! I also pray aloud and that aids my concentration as well as my voice.

Likewise, if I am last in a queue in a supermarket, I will often chat to those who serve me at the till. For example, I know quite a lot about one of the older assistants at our local foodstore: she has a dog, two sons, a daughter and her husband is an architect! Young assistants, often students working part-time, respond to being asked what their hopes and ambitions are, and appreciate interest being shown in them. What is more, I have used my voice and made friends!

A challenging instrument

The tongue is that part of our human body that can do the most good or the most harm. James urges, 'do not slander one another' (4:11). Gossiping, malicious talk and saying things that ought not to be said at all come naturally to fallen human nature. When we hear something bad of another person, the instinctive reaction often is to think, 'There's no smoke without fire.' However, to slander is to imitate the evil one, whose name *diabolos* means 'slanderer'. It belongs to our old life and we need to be rid of it (Eph. 4:31;

Jas. 1:21). Not only will our fellowship with God be hindered by it, but it will ruin our testimony to the saving power of our Lord Jesus Christ.

One group of Christians can easily slip into the snare of slandering another, especially if they are of a different denomination or have a varying emphasis on some secondary point of doctrine. We need to be on our guard whenever we hear the question, 'Have you heard what is going on at present at such and such a church?'

In contrast, words can have the ability to build up, stimulate and encourage. Many are weighed down by responsibilities. Human relationships are sometimes in chaos, and kind words have not been the norm. Consequently there are broken marriages, families and lives. Our privilege is to share our Saviour's invitation: 'Come to me, all you who are weary and burdened, and I will give you rest' (Matt. 11:28). Many days provide the opportunity to use words to encourage someone.

A unique type of talking

We referred earlier to an unrivalled kind of talking: 'Then those who feared the LORD talked with each other, and the LORD listened and heard. A scroll of remembrance was written in his presence concerning those who feared the LORD and honoured his name' (Mal. 3:16). Believers possess a remarkable fellowship through talking together of the Lord whom they delight to honour. At the centre of their conversation is the Lord Himself: what He has done for them, and all that He is to them. By talking together about Him, our souls are refreshed, and our determination to honour Him is renewed and strengthened.

There is another unique type of talking: talking to yourself! I am not suggesting that it is something you do in public! But it is a good habit in a number of ways.

Psalm 103 begins with David talking to his soul: 'Praise the LORD, O my soul; all my inmost being, praise his holy name.' After meditating on God's character, David ends the psalm by talking to himself again: 'Praise the LORD, O my soul' (Ps. 103:22). We have reason to do the same.

Psalms 42 and 43 illustrate the psalmist talking to himself when depressed: 'Why are you downcast, O my soul? Why so disturbed within me?' On three occasions the same question is asked (42:5, 11; 43:5). After each he exercises his mind in remembering

God's goodness to him in the past, resulting in praise and renewed trust in God (42:11; 43:5).

Preaching on Psalm 42, Dr Martyn Lloyd-Jones asked, 'Have you realised that most of your unhappiness in life is due to the fact that you are listening to yourself instead of talking to yourself?'[11] If I am honest, I can feel sorry for myself when my legs hurt, probably on account of my old age, diabetes and, perhaps, medication that I am on. Then is the time to talk to myself: 'Hold on a bit! You have had those legs for a long time, longer than anyone would drive the same car! Think of when you were able to walk and run. Think of the disabled people you know.' After talking to myself, I feel altogether different – I am filled with thankfulness and the desire to pray for others who have much more to contend with than I do.

Why is talking so important in old age?

- It will be honouring to God if people remember us when we die for the good things we have said rather than the bad.
- In few areas of life can we be more of an

example or encouragement than when we speak with a God-instructed tongue.

- It is a great privilege to encourage others: 'Gold there is, and rubies in abundance, but lips that speak knowledge are a rare jewel' (Prov. 20:15).

A PRAYER FOR OUR SPEECH AND TALKING

Please help me, Lord, so to fill my heart with the good things of Your Word that my tongue may share and speak about them when the opportunity is present. May the talk that comes out of my mouth be always helpful and beneficial to others and may I be quicker to listen than to speak. Teach me how to speak timely and gentle words. I ask these things in Jesus' Name. Amen.

U IS FOR UNDERSTAND

One of the benefits of old age ought to be increased wisdom and understanding. But that is not true to experience because life can be a record of failures, mistakes and the sorrow they have brought. But thank God that even through these sadnesses we may have learned important lessons that we can share with others. As old people, we ought to be channels of God's wisdom as we care about the generations that follow us and share the lessons God has taught us both in our successes and our failures.

We have mentioned already the importance of our praying for the work and witness of God's people who are now fulfilling the tasks and functions that once were ours, but I want to emphasise once more that praying is one of the most important things that we do. Let me give you a couple of examples.

In the early twentieth century some women in the Scottish borders felt a burden for Charlotte Chapel, a church in Edinburgh that was desperately in need of a pastor. They prayed earnestly over a long period of time, little knowing how their prayer was going to be answered. Wonderfully their petition was granted: not only in the arrival of a pastor, Joseph Kemp, but in the revival he was to see in Edinburgh – as he reported on his visit to Wales at the time of the revival there in 1904.

Likewise, three retired ministers belonged to a local church. During a vacancy in the leadership they were concerned that the man appointed should be someone whose ministry would be faithful to God's Word and the gospel of the Lord Jesus. They covenanted to meet together regularly to pray that the right man would come. Their prayers were answered, although probably the other church members knew nothing of their covenant.

In addition to grasping the pre-eminence of prayer, we also need to understand the following principles.

Understand that, old as we are, we should still be growing in the grace and knowledge of our Lord Jesus Christ

While we have stopped growing physically, we are not to stop growing spiritually – no matter how great our age (2 Pet. 3:18). Paul expresses well the ambition that should mark all our life when he writes, 'whatever was to my profit I now consider loss for the sake of Christ. What is more, I consider everything a loss compared to the surpassing greatness of knowing Christ Jesus my Lord' (Phil. 3:7–8).

Understand that the Scriptures are to be our unfailing guide until our life's end

Ways of doing things will always be changing, and sometimes we may be puzzled by them, but the solution is to check them by the truth God imparts by His Word. Change has always challenged Christians throughout the centuries and they have had to weigh up in their minds and hearts the principles by which they should judge their actions and attitudes. We may often discover that our objections to change cannot be justified. Do not be ashamed of acknowledging that fact: 'Whoever loves discipline loves knowledge, but he who hates correction is stupid' (Prov. 12:1).

Understand the pressures and challenges faced by the generations following us

Families are a precious gift from God for which we should daily thank Him. We may fall into the snare sometimes of thinking that we do not see much of them, or that they could be doing more for us. But beware! That may be the first step towards spoiling our relationship with them. I remember when all four of our children were at school how busy my wife and I used to be: transporting them to different activities; trying to give them quality time; and endeavouring not to forget our duty to our own parents, especially when they lived on their own after bereavement.

Understand others by sympathising with what you know of their difficult circumstances and challenges

Thinking of the people round about me where I live or my friends whom I meet in church week by week, I am aware of the loneliness of some. Others face the challenge of caring for a marriage partner who has dementia or Parkinson's disease or cancer. Then the radio and television news daily brings heart-rending stories of refugees and victims of war. As I think of these individuals, the writer of the letter to the Hebrews urges understanding that leads to intelligent prayer: 'Remember those in prison *as if you were* their fellow-prisoners, and those who are ill-treated *as if you yourselves* were suffering' (Heb. 13:3, my italics).

Understand that increasing limitations and frustrations are inevitable in old age

I thought I was old when I retired because things I had once found easy to do became difficult. But, twenty years later, challenges have been increasing almost imperceptibly to the extent that now I cannot go out without a walking stick; I cannot run to get a bus; I cannot climb a ladder to reach something; I cannot cut my own toenails; much as I love talking to people, I find that it takes a lot out of me. But hold on, I must remember the God-given counsel of 1 Thessalonians 5:16: 'Be joyful always; pray continually; give thanks in all circumstances, for this is God's will for you in Christ Jesus.' Yes, I can do all those things through my Saviour who strengthens me. What a lot I have for which to be thankful! The challenge to us all is what kind of face do we present to our contemporaries as well as to those much younger? Doleful or Cheerful?

Understand that – just as in every stage of life – when dealing with every problem or challenge we face, we are be guided by the Scriptures

As Paul wrote, 'All Scripture is God-breathed and is useful for teaching, rebuking, correcting and training in righteousness' (2 Tim. 3:16). Therefore, for every stage and challenge of life, the Bible provides guidance and we should daily look for it there.

Understanding is a benefit to cherish: 'He who gets wisdom loves his own soul; he who cherishes understanding prospers' (Prov. 19:8) – and there is no age restriction!

Truths to shape our understanding in old age

- One day our understanding will be perfect: 'Now we see but a poor reflection as in a mirror; then we shall see face to face. Now I know in part; then I shall know fully, even as I am fully known' (1 Cor. 13:12).
- Meanwhile, understand that the most important service is often that which is unseen.
- None can better help old people to come to faith than other old people.

- Do not underestimate the knowledge God gives you through His Word. The humblest believer who studies the Bible with the help of God's Spirit may be wiser in understanding than a Professor of Theology who depends upon his own intelligence.

AN ANONYMOUS PRAYER FOR A LIFE OF SERVICE

God be in my head
And in my understanding;
God be in my eyes
And in my looking;
God be in my mouth
And in my speaking;
God be in my heart
And in my thinking;
God be at my end
And in my departing.
Amen.

V IS FOR VICTORIOUS

When I was young, victorious Christian living was much spoken of and preached on. Perhaps it sometimes went to extremes of suggesting the possibility of living a life of sinless perfection, which is clearly not the Bible's teaching. New birth brings about our release from the kingdom of darkness over which Satan reigns to belong instead to God's kingdom of light, but it results in constant endeavours on Satan's part to sabotage our obedience to God.

We are in a spiritual battle

We engage in a spiritual battle from the moment of our new birth until our death and entry into God's presence. Traditionally, it has been described as a fight against the world, the flesh and the devil, and that definition sums up the fight in which we are engaged – and as much when we are old as when we were young.

We are fighting worldliness

The fight against the world is the fight against worldliness. That is to say, the battle is not allowing our thinking to be moulded by the spirit of the age in which we live. Rather it is acting according to the life of practical holiness to which God calls us from the moment of our new birth. Much contemporary television, film, theatre and culture in general do not portray good and healthy subjects or objectives upon which it is spiritually and morally profitable to think about and emulate. Rather it is all too often dwelling upon what is sordid, revealing human nature at its worst.

Therefore, when faced with any form of entertainment, I find it is good to ask myself, can I honesty pray for God's blessing upon my doing this as I can when I meet with God's people on His day and bow my head in prayer? Many television 'soaps', comedy shows, and contemporary portrayal of classical literature tend to focus on the baser elements of human nature. While there is no doubt about the reality of such elements, it is not helpful to enjoy being entertained by them.

Instead, the Holy Spirit would lead us in paths of righteousness.

This fight against the flesh is described in Romans 7, where Paul admits his own experience – which, if we are honest, mirrors our own: 'I do not understand what I do. For what I want to do I do not do, but what I hate I do … For I have the desire to do what is good, but I cannot carry it out' (vv. 15, 18). This battle against the sins of my flesh continues in old age, and the victory is only gained – as in earlier years – by our honest confession of sin when we fall and by our looking to God for His grace and power to overcome sin. We are victorious only as we fix our eyes upon the Lord Jesus and aim at obedience to God's will and law as we read the Scriptures day by day.

We are opposing the devil's lies

One of the cleverest things the devil has done is to encourage people to make fun of his reality. Instead of positively resisting him, so that he flees from us (Jas. 4:7), we fall into his traps and snares. His power is so great that our Lord Jesus prayed against him on behalf of all who become His disciples (John 17:15). The enemy of souls discerns our weakest points and makes his attack there. There are occasions when the devil directs particular attacks upon us – Paul refers to 'the day of evil' that often dawns (Eph. 6:13).

The devil will use 'flaming arrows' that have as their aim our abandoning faith as a basic principle of our life. He will try to introduce doubts about God's reality or faithfulness. He will encourage slackness in prayer and discourage boldness in witness. Yet every time we are aware of temptation we should immediately call upon God and then we may be sure that 'he will come near' to deliver us (Jas. 4:8).

God intends us to be victorious

One of the most helpful passages in the Bible concerning living victoriously is Ephesians 6:10–20, where we find the spiritual armour essential for daily victory:

- Our principal aim is to stand up against the devil's schemes and to withstand his attacks (v. 11).
- Our strength is in the Lord and His mighty power as we put on the spiritual armour He provides (v. 10).
- This equipment is only effective as we put every piece on; with it all on we will be able to stand our ground against Satan and the temptations he puts in our way to trip us up (v. 13)

- We must be truthful in admitting, confessing and identifying our temptations (v. 14). To fight Satan we must begin with truth – what David describes as 'truth in the inner parts' (Ps. 51:6). How comfortable do we find it to be honest with ourselves before God? How easy is it to be honest when we have done something wrong, and something of which we know we ought to be ashamed?

- We must truthfully admit these things to God and then do what we know is right (v. 14). If we fail to do what we know is right in anything, we leave a chink in our armour that immediately Satan will seize. We must, therefore, put on 'the breastplate of righteousness'.

- As soon as we do this, we will find we have the gospel shoes on, making us ready to bear witness to our Saviour (v. 15).

- We will discover afresh the power of God's salvation and our trust in Him renewed so that we prove the effectiveness of our two spiritually powerful weapons – the sword of God's Word (v. 17) and the unseen weapon of prayer (v. 18).

As often as I get dressed each morning, I need to put in place this armour!

Specific areas where I need to be victorious in old age

- Overcoming temptations to self-pity that accompany daily limitations and frustrations.
- Overcoming unhelpful talking of 'the good old days'!
- Forgetting the truth that whatever difficulties old age brings to us, God intends that we should be 'more than conquerors through him who loved us' (Rom. 8:37).

A PRAYER FOR VICTORY OVER TEMPTATION

Heavenly Father, I want to bow in Your presence, and acknowledge those areas of my life where I fail most often and where I am most vulnerable to failure. Thank You that, with my eyes upon the Lord Jesus, I may confidently say, 'I can overcome every challenge to my faith and obedience through Him who gives me strength.' Amen.

W IS FOR WALK

How recognisable are you by your walk? We all are, although perhaps some more than others. Once I was watching the first day of a cricket Test Match when, during the lunch break, a man walked down the aisle. Like a shot I called out, 'Amos!' He turned towards me and, yes, it was Amos, someone with whom I had been at school many years before! If you had asked me exactly how he walked I could not have told you, but it was such a distinctive way of walking that my memory was jogged and I recognised him by his walk!

Enoch's distinctiveness is that he is the first person of whom it is recorded that he 'walked with God' (Gen. 5:24). He began life out of step with God, just like us, but he came to realise there was a choice he had to make – a choice of faith. He believed not only that God exists but also that God 'rewards those who earnestly seek him' (Heb. 11:6).

It was a choice determined by desire for no one walks with God unwillingly. God never forces His fellowship upon His creatures. No doubt Enoch expressed a hunger and desire for such an experience as he prayed. Sadly, others did not do the same. He was prepared to swim against the tide.

A major theme of the Old Testament

Psalm 1 is the foundation of all the other psalms and significantly begins, 'Blessed is the man who *does not walk in the counsel of the wicked* or stand in the way of sinners, or sit in the seat of mockers. But his delight is in the law of the LORD, and on his law he meditates day and night' (vv. 1–2, my italics). Walking with God does not mean isolation from the world around us; rather it is separation from the world's ungodly thinking, behaviour and attitudes.

God asks, through the prophet Amos, 'Do two walk together unless they have agreed to do so?' (3:3). If we would walk with God, we must first agree with His purpose for our life: He made us for Himself so that in youth or old age we might live for Him and bring Him praise.

The New Testament's equal emphasis upon the priority of our 'walk'

The often overlooked secret of the early church's growth and development was that it enjoyed a period of rest from persecution after Paul's conversion so that 'walking in the fear of the Lord, and in the comfort of the Holy Ghost, [they] were multiplied' (Acts 9:31, KJV). To walk with God implies agreement, familiarity and affection for Him, and something that is habitual.

Our walk should bear the following characteristics.

We are to walk in love

Love must characterise our Christian way of living (Eph. 5:2) for love is the foremost aspect of the Holy Spirit's fruit in our life. We cannot be in step with God and at the same time out of harmony with God's people. Our equal concern will be for good relationships with those who are not yet Christians (Col. 4:5).

We are to walk by faith

We are to follow the examples of Enoch and all the heroes of the faith (Heb. 12:1–2). The secret is fixing our eyes upon the Lord Jesus, something the Holy

Spirit delights to help us do as we seek His help.

The way to indescribable blessings

We have seen that we are to be obedient in walking in love and faith as commanded by Scripture. It is also, however, the means by which we benefit in wonderful aspects.

Fellowship

The foremost benefit of walking with God is the enjoyment of fellowship with Him. In human relationships we enjoy walking with someone, sharing each other's company and getting to know one another. So it is as we walk with God our Saviour, Jesus Christ, who delights to reveal more of Himself to us (John 14:21).

Strength

From fellowship comes strength. Walking with God we may lean upon Him, and find Him just when and where we need Him: 'those who hope in the LORD will renew their strength. They will soar on wings like eagles; they will run and not grow weary, they will walk and not be faint' (Is. 40:31).

Joy

In walking with God we discover joy, and sometimes an unspeakable joy. We may walk with Him in loneliness, in illness, in difficulty and in every demanding situation, and find ourselves inwardly satisfied. As such we may echo these words: 'Whom have I in heaven but you? And earth has nothing I desire besides you' (Ps. 73:25). Such is the testimony of someone who walks with God.

Fruitfulness

Walking with God, we also become fruitful. Psalm 1, to which we have already referred, speaks of the fruitfulness of the person who walks with God. God Himself is the source of all true fruitfulness. Our Lord Jesus says to us, as to His first disciples, 'apart from me you can do nothing' (John 15:5).

Have you noticed that when two people live harmoniously together, they so often become like one another in character and behaviour? Walking with the Lord Jesus we become more like Him.

Guidance

As we walk with God, we may trust Him to take us and guide us in the way He wants us to go. With that thought in mind, I find myself at ease praying the last verse of an old hymn in the Sankey-Moody hymnbook:

So on I go not knowing,
I would not if I might;
I'd rather walk in the dark with God
Than go alone in the light;
I'd rather walk by faith with Him
Than go alone by sight.

(Mary Gardiner Brainard)[12]

A taste of heaven

Walking with God becomes increasingly a foretaste of heaven. Heaven was in Enoch before he was in heaven! It was said of General Gordon, 'He literally walked with God, and if it were not disrespectful, one might also say arm in arm with Him.'[13]

Why is walking with God so important in old age?

- On a day when I may see no one, but am walking with God and knowing His smile, I can smile.

- Christians who walk with God easily recognise one another. It is a family characteristic!
- I want to leave a godly example to family, friends and neighbours that will be a help and encouragement to them.
- I want to be ready at any moment for God to say to me, as He did to Enoch, 'It is time for you to come home.'

A PRAYER FOR
A CLOSER WALK WITH GOD

O for a closer walk with God,
A calm and heavenly frame,
A light to shine upon the road
That leads me to the Lamb! …

The dearest idol I have known,
Whate'er that idol be,
Help me to tear it from thy throne
And worship only thee.

So shall my walk be close with God,
Calm and serene my frame;

So purer light shall mark the road
That leads me to the Lamb.

(William Cowper)[14]

X IS FOR
THE X FACTOR

I would not be surprised if, before reading our first chapter, you looked up what the letter X represents! The term 'X factor' seems to have first been used in 1934 when scientists became aware that there existed an answer to a blood problem which they had not yet found but the existence of which they were certain. (It had to do with discovering that the drug heparin helps to prevent the formation of blood clots.) They called it the X factor!

The X factor of the Christian faith is the exciting good news that our Lord Jesus Christ provides the only answer to the sad reality we and people everywhere face – the awful and sobering prospect of death and God's rightful judgment upon us. Living as I do in a small community of thirty flats and bungalows, there has not been a year without a death, some completely unexpected. But the subject of death is almost taboo.

The vital intervention of our Lord Jesus Christ

Our Lord Jesus Christ came 'to shine on those living in darkness and in the shadow of death' (Luke 1:79). To bring that light which overcomes death's darkness was unspeakably costly to Him.

It meant, first, His incarnation – He took upon Himself our human flesh in order to become the Sin-Bearer. He, the just, died for the unjust to bring us to God. He took upon Himself the penalty of death that our sin deserves, although He had never sinned, so that God's punishment of sin might not be inflicted upon us.

On the third day He rose again, to be the Resurrection and the Life for all who put their trust in Him. The Greek word for life – *zoe* – is reserved in the Bible for eternal, never-ending life: God's life. Jesus declared, 'I am the resurrection and the life. He who believes in me will live, even though he dies; and whoever lives and believes in me will never die' (John 11:25–26). Some years later the apostle John affirmed, 'And this is the testimony: God has given us eternal life, and this life is in his Son. He who has the Son has life; he who does not have the Son of God does not have life' (1 John 5:11–12).

Death abolished!

The Resurrection provided visible proof of our Saviour's victory. It also gave evidence of what God will do for us when our trust is in His Son as our Saviour. Our bodies will be raised like His.

We will be as recognisable as He was. At the same time we will have a body suitable for eternity for, as Paul explains,

> *When you sow, you do not plant the body that will be, but just a seed, perhaps of wheat or of something else. But God gives it a body as he has determined ... The body that is sown is perishable, it is raised imperishable; it is sown in dishonour, it is raised in glory; it is sown in weakness, it is raised in power; it is sown a natural body, it is raised a spiritual body (1 Cor. 15:37–38, 42–44).*

Death is said to 'belong' to those who belong to Christ (1 Cor. 3:22, NASB). If something belongs to us, we do not have to be afraid of it. Death is simply a change of address – and to a better address! It is going home, since the Lord Jesus said, 'In my Father's house are many rooms; if it were not so, I would have told you. I am going there to prepare a place for you' (John 14:2). It is to be present with the Lord.

We can serve our own generations and those that follow by being ready to talk of Jesus' victory over death, and by giving a reason for the hope that is within us. When a death occurs, it is not inappropriate to ask thoughtful questions. Let me suggest a few it is opportune to ask ourselves or others when we hear of someone's death:

- Are we ready to face our Maker?
- Have you thought of the hymns you would like to be sung at your funeral?
- Have you left instructions for your family as to the arrangements when you die?

Obviously initiating such questions and comments must be done thoughtfully and sensitively, but we need to be ready to give the reasons we have for the assurance that death can be the path to life through our Lord Jesus.

The importance of honesty

This glorious assurance of the Christian's spiritual birthright does not mean that all fears about death disappear. Remember the enemy of souls, the devil, may – indeed will – aim his fiery darts at us, trying not only to distress us but to sow seeds of doubt into the hearts and minds of those close to us. The last verse of William Williams' hymn is an appropriate prayer:

> *When I tread the verge of Jordan,*
> *Bid my anxious fears subside;*
> *Death of deaths, and hell's destruction,*
> *Land me safe on Canaan's side.*
> *Songs of praises, songs of praises,*
> *I will ever give to Thee;*
> *I will ever give to Thee.*[15]

Why is the X factor so important in old age?

- The assurance of the forgiveness of my sins and God's gift of eternal life through my Saviour's saving work on my behalf are my most precious possessions.
- I cannot honour the Lord Jesus more than by sharing and declaring the good news He has made possible.
- Daily I live and meet daily people who are

spiritually dead, as once I was, with no assurance of heaven.

• A day is wasted when I do not think of death and realise my urgent need to pray for my family and friends that they may know and live in the reality of John 3:16: 'For God so loved the world that he gave his one and only Son, that whoever believes in him shall not perish but have eternal life.'

A PRAYER FOR GOD'S HELP IN SHARING THE X FACTOR

Father, as I bow before You, I recognise that in Your Son You have shown us the way to eternal life, a life the wonders of which cannot be fully expressed or explained in words. I want to name before You now relatives, friends and neighbours who do not yet understand this good news and who show no inclination to do so ... Help me not to neglect praying for them and being ready at any moment to give a reason for the glorious assurance I have for the future through our Lord Jesus. In His Name I pray. Amen.

Y IS FOR YEARN

Think of a flowering plant. In the middle is an artificial flower, perfectly resembling real flowers. Then remember two things: first, the live flowers yearn for water. Second, as you water them, in proportion to what they regularly need, they will grow, whereas the artificial flower remains exactly the same.

Now place the plant in a window where the sun may shine upon them. Their heads will bend towards the sun; if you turn the plant around so that other flowers are in sight of the sun, they will do the same. The artificial flower, however, will remain erect with no desire for the sun.

This is like the difference between a soul that is dead and one that is alive. A flower yearns for water and a glimpse of the sun. A soul made alive through the salvation that is in our Saviour yearns for Him and the glimpses the Holy Spirit gives of Him to every soul that looks towards Him.

Yearn for God's fellowship

Wonderfully God yearns for our fellowship before ever we yearn for His! Then, at our new birth, His Spirit actually comes to live within us, enabling us to cry, 'Abba, Father!' My hope is that even now we will feel within us the promptings of His Spirit to seek God's face, expressing our yearnings after fellowship with Him.

One of the many blessings of reading through the Book of Psalms regularly is that they show us – and even give us the words – to express our yearnings after God. For example, David declares, 'the LORD God is a sun ...' (Ps. 84:11). As people enjoy 'sunning' themselves, so we may enjoy 'sunning' ourselves in His presence.

This same idea of delighting in God is expressed in one of Frances Ridley Havergal's hymns, the first verse of which is:

Sit down beneath His shadow,
And rest with great delight;
The faith that now beholds Him
Is pledge of future sight.[16]

Yearn for spiritual milk

You and I probably entered adulthood when it was not the practice for husbands to be present at the birth of their children. When my wife was in labour, I remember the midwife ushering me out of our bedroom! But I recall waiting downstairs to hear the sign of birth – a baby's cry! One of the first thing a baby does is to cry desiring its mother's milk. In a similar way Peter urges his readers, 'Like newborn babies, crave pure spiritual milk, so that by it you may grow up in your salvation, now that you have tasted that the Lord is good' (1 Pet. 2:2–3). As milk is the primary source of nutrition for infants before they are able to digest other types of food, so God's Word feeds our longings after God, and we should expect it to be the case.

How good is our spiritual appetite? When we go to church, do we ask the Lord to speak to us personally by what is taught and preached? Is our daily time of prayer and Bible reading the best part of the day?

Yearn for the salvation of those who are lost, as once we were

Just as we have tasted the delights of being saved and becoming part of God's family, so we should desire for others to know this same reality. As the Lord Jesus looked out upon the crowds who pursued Him to hear what He taught, Matthew writes, 'he had compassion on them, because they were harassed and helpless, like sheep without a shepherd' (9:36). We too need to care for the spiritually lost.

Yearn for fellowship with fellow believers

Always keep yourself in fellowship with God's people. As we get older, we are not able to meet with others as once we did, but there are things we can do to help us compensate for this. Let me suggest just three. First, invite both young and old to visit you. Second, meet regularly with a Christian friend with the deliberate intention of talking together about the Lord, and sharing encouragements you have received as you have read the Scriptures. Third, use one evening a week – especially perhaps on a Sunday evening – to be in touch by phone with other older people who may not get out.

Yearn after the future God has promised us

Satan encourages bad habits and two in particular with great subtlety. The first is not to talk much about the Lord Jesus and the second is not to talk about heaven and the life to come in glory. We should be yearning for heaven for that is the place where our Saviour is and where He prepares a place for us. God – here and now – is preparing us in advance for glory (Rom. 9:23). What an amazing description and thought!

Ponder our Lord Jesus' prayer, not long before His death, resurrection and ascension: 'Father, I want those you have given me to be with me where I am, and to see my glory, the glory you have given me because you loved me before the creation of the world' (John 17:24). No wonder Christians should yearn for heaven – especially those of us whose journey of life has been long and nears its conclusion.

Paul wrote, 'For to me, to live is Christ and to die is gain. If I am to go on living in the body, this will mean fruitful labour for me. Yet what shall I choose? I do not know! I am torn between the two: I desire to depart and be with Christ, which is better by far' (Phil. 1:21–23).

Identify and put right everything you know that diminishes your yearning

Books that we read and films or television programmes we watch all have the capacity to sow the seeds of backsliding in our hearts, taking our love for God off the boil. Likewise our love fades if we fail to seek and enjoy fellowship with other Christians, or experience the breakdown of human relationships through quarrels and disagreements which we have failed to put right.

Know that God yearns for you!

A glorious and amazing truth is that if, as God's children, we do not yearn after Him, He – amazingly, graciously and tenderly – yearns for our undivided devotion (Jas. 4:5)! He longs that we might drink daily from the wells of salvation always open to us (Is. 12:3).

A PRAYER FOR
THE RIGHT KIND OF YEARNING

Heavenly Father, help me to take in the truth that You yearn for fellowship with Your children. Thank You for every yearning I have after fellowship with You, prompted so faithfully by the Holy Spirit. May my appreciation of Your Word and the daily privilege of prayer increase, becoming more and more my delight, so that I grow in the grace and knowledge of our Lord and Saviour Jesus Christ, in whose Name I pray. Amen.

Z IS FOR ZEAL

It is appropriate that the last letter of our alphabet should be zeal. In old age physical ability, mobility and opportunities to be involved in activities that have been a lifetime's delight diminish. But old age should not mean a lessening of zeal for knowing God and doing His will.

Good and bad zeal

Zeal has a bad press this century where thousands suffer through the evil acts of violent extremists, fired by a false zeal for their cause. Prior to Paul's meeting with the Lord Jesus on the Damascus road, he too persecuted the followers of Jesus to their death through a mistaken zeal.

Zeal is like fire – a wonderful servant but a dreadful master: 'It is not good to have zeal without knowledge, nor to be hasty and miss the way' (Prov. 19:2). Bad zeal springs from ignorance, bigotry, prejudice, narrow-mindedness and intolerance. It prompts hasty judgments and violence in words and actions. Behind its abuse is the enemy of our souls.

Yet that zeal can be good is clear because God speaks in Scripture of His own zeal, and nowhere more than in the promise of the first coming of our Saviour into the world: 'The zeal of the LORD Almighty will accomplish this' (Is. 9:7). When the disciples witnessed Jesus' righteous cleansing of the temple, they remembered words from the Old Testament: 'zeal for your house consumes me' (Ps. 69:9; cf. John 2:17).

The best guide to zeal

The Lord's Prayer uniquely pinpoints areas of life where we should be zealous (Matt. 6:9–13).

Zeal for fellowship with our Heavenly Father

No privilege is greater than calling God 'our Father'. Prayer is not simply asking God for things; it is wanting to be in His presence. Let us be zealous for fellowship with our Heavenly Father! He waits for His children to call upon Him.

Zeal for the honour of God's Name

We rightly cringe with shame when we hear His Name taken in vain in blasphemy. David wrote,

'My zeal wears me out, for my enemies ignore your words' (Ps. 119:139). As Paul wandered Athens' streets, he was distressed to see that the city was so full of idols (Acts 17:16) and his zeal for God's Name meant that he could not keep silent.

Zeal for the coming of God's kingdom

God's kingdom is first of all His reign or rule in our life. Second, it is the kingdom of which Christians are members because the Lord Jesus Christ actively rules as King in their hearts. Third, it is the kingdom that Christians possess as a future inheritance. Zeal for the coming of God's kingdom should spur us to live to advance it and see its wonderful fruition.

Zeal that God's will should be done

Before the revelation of God's everlasting kingdom, the gospel of His Son is to be preached to every nation, people and tribe. We are to be zealous in our support of God's work both where we live and through those who represent us throughout the world.

Zeal for contentment and practical action for the needy

Our relative affluence may cause us to take our daily

bread for granted. We may think more of what we would like to add to our possessions rather than what we might zealously share sacrificially with the needy.

Zeal for right relationships
This means never finishing a day with unforgiveness in our hearts. That may involve a late-night phone call or a message sent to the person against whom we have harboured a grudge. He or she may respond by saying, 'I apologise too.' Whatever is the case, we will be able to sleep with a right relationship to our Heavenly Father. We honour God's Name when our forgiveness of others is modelled on His forgiveness of us.

Zeal for fighting the good fight of faith
The Lord's Prayer ends, 'And lead us not into temptation, but deliver us from the evil one.' Never minimise the reality or subtlety of 'your enemy the devil' who 'prowls around like a roaring lion looking for someone to devour' (1 Pet. 5:8). Be daily zealous for the well-being of your soul in its relationship to God.

An Old Testament theme
An interesting discovery I have made is that

zeal is spoken of in the Bible more than I first thought! I wonder if you have ever wondered if there is value in reading the long lists of names found in the Old Testament? Read Nehemiah 3:20. One man stood out for the zeal with which he did work in God's Name, building a wall while never knowing that it was going to be noticed and written about! We do not need to be in a position of power to be commended for acting out of zeal for God's honour.

A New Testament imperative

Having unfolded the wonders, glories and blessings of the gospel in the first eleven chapters of his letter to the Romans, Paul begins chapter twelve with the important word – 'therefore'. Among the imperatives that follow are the words of verse 11: 'Never be lacking in zeal, but keep your spiritual fervour' (Rom. 12:11). If we are obedient to God's Spirit, we will be sensitive to those things that will increase our spiritual fervour and those that do the opposite – particularly how we spend our free time, the books we choose to read, the programmes we watch on television, and the subjects we choose to talk about with our friends and family.

Why should zeal appear in An A–Z of Old Age?

- If I have grown spiritually in Christ, my zeal will be far greater now than it was when first I came to know Him.
- While not physically active as once I was, that should be no hindrance to my spiritual zeal as I daily share my life with my Lord and Saviour as the ever welcome guest in my life.
- Christian fellowship, as it ought to be, is contagious and refines and feeds our souls: 'As iron sharpens iron, so one man sharpens another' (Prov. 27:17).

A PRAYER FOR ZEAL

Gracious Father, grant me honesty as I examine my zeal. Help me to be as zealous as possible for someone of my age for the coming of Your Son and the revelation of Your everlasting kingdom. Deliver me from all lukewarmness in my fellowship with You, and with Your people. May I always be hot and never cold in talking about Your Son and sharing the good news of salvation. I ask for these benefits in Jesus' Name. Amen.

REFERENCES

1   George Herbert, 'The Elixir' (1633).
2   Edward Mote, 'My hope is built on nothing less' (1834).
3   Thomas Kelly, 'Praise the Saviour, ye who know Him' (1806).
4   William Cowper, 'What various hindrances we meet' (1779).
5   John Newton, 'How sweet the Name of Jesus sounds' (1779).
6   Thomas Brooks, found in *The Ultimate Puritan Collection* (Amazon Kindle edition).
7   John H. Sammis, 'When we walk with the Lord' (1887).
8   https://hymnary.org/hymn/CHB41972/731
9   Howard Taylor, Dr & Mrs, *Hudson Taylor and The China Inland Mission* (C.I.M, 1946) p.169
10 www.goodreads.com/quotes/12757

[11] Lloyd-Jones, Dr M, *Spiritual Depression, its Causes and Cures* (Pickering and Inglis Ltd, 1974) p.20-21

[12] Mary Gardiner Brainard, 'I know not what awaits me' (1869).

[13] John Pollock, *Gordon: The man behind the legend* (Lion Books, new edition 1995).

[14] William Cowper, 'O for a closer walk with God' (1772).

[15] William Williams, 'Guide me, O Thou great Jehovah' (1745).

[16] Frances Ridley Havergal, 'Sit down beneath His shadow' (1852).